NATIONAL (UN)BELONGING

Studies in Critical Social Sciences Book Series

Haymarket Books is proud to be working with Brill Academic Publishers (www.brill.nl) to republish the *Studies in Critical Social Sciences* book series in paperback editions. This peer-reviewed book series offers insights into our current reality by exploring the content and consequences of power relationships under capitalism, and by considering the spaces of opposition and resistance to these changes that have been defining our new age. Our full catalog of *SCSS* volumes can be viewed at https://www.haymarketbooks .org/series_collections/4-studies-in-critical-social-sciences.

NATIONAL (UN)BELONGING

Bengali American Women on Imagining and
Contesting Culture and Identity

ROKSANA BADRUDDOJA

Haymarket Books
Chicago, IL

First published in 2022 by Brill Academic Publishers, The Netherlands
© 2022 Koninklijke Brill NV, Leiden, The Netherlands

Published in paperback in 2023 by
Haymarket Books
P.O. Box 180165
Chicago, IL 60618
773-583-7884
www.haymarketbooks.org

ISBN: 979-8-88890-008-6

Distributed to the trade in the US through Consortium Book Sales and
Distribution (www.cbsd.com) and internationally through Ingram Publisher
Services International (www.ingramcontent.com).

This book was published with the generous support of Lannan Foundation,
Wallace Action Fund, and the Marguerite Casey Foundation.

Special discounts are available for bulk purchases by organizations and
institutions. Please call 773-583-7884 or email info@haymarketbooks.org for more
information.

Cover design by Jamie Kerry and Ragina Johnson.

Printed in the United States.

Library of Congress Cataloging-in-Publication data is available.

To Raneem, Sarayu, Munay, and Nyctea ... You All Belong

∵

Contents

Foreword: Telling America's Whole Story

When I became Director of the Smithsonian Institution's Asian Pacific American Program, the mission was clear: America's whole story had yet to be told at the world's largest museum and research complex, consisting of nineteen museums and galleries, the National Zoological Park, and nine research facilities. Established in 1997, the Asian Pacific American Program produces programs and exhibitions about the Asian Pacific American experience, and works in partnership with museums, galleries, and research centers to enrich Smithsonian collections and activities. Despite a number of successful programs, exhibitions, and acquisitions, the history, art, and culture of Asian Pacific Americans remain underrepresented at the Smithsonian, especially when considered in relation to the voices represented in Smithsonian museums, such as the National Museum of the American Indian and the National Museum of African American History and Culture, and in relation to well-resourced initiatives, such as the proposal to build a Smithsonian National Museum of the American Latino, the Smithsonian Latino Center, and the Smithsonian Latino Initiatives Pool Fund. Setting aside the issue of building stand-alone museums of heritage, the drive to recognize American Indians, African Americans, Latinos, and Asian Pacific Americans in the nation's museum and research complex affirms the dignity of America and Americans. This important task, however, inevitably raises questions about how one can represent a multi- and inter-racial, cultural, ethnic, and generational story of America. To direct this question towards the work of the Smithsonian Asian Pacific American Program, how can Asian Pacific America insert itself in a story in which the Asian Pacific American experience has a fuller role to play? What do the voices of Asian Pacific American history, art, and culture have to say?

It is tempting to present the Asian Pacific American experience solely through celebratory voices, supporting a conventional immigrant tale of assimilation and achievement. It is less contentious to understand Asian Pacific America via the insertion of Asian Pacific American voices as witnesses to, and evidence of, American exceptionalism in a world of free and democratic societies. However, telling America's whole story is also guided by the critical movements that established and institutionalized the field of Ethnic Studies in the late 1960s and early 1970s, as the next step in the march for civil rights. In my own field of research—Asian Pacific American cinema and digital media—the activism foundational to Ethnic Studies led to the formation of community-based Asian Pacific American film organizations dedicated to empowering Asian Pacific American voices through film and television. Coalitions of activists, scholars, and artists across the country created historic organizations such as Los Angeles's Visual Communications (1971), New York City's Asian CineVision (1976), and San Francisco's Center for Asian American Media (1980). These organizations represented the call for Asian Pacific American representations through Asian Pacific American voices.

There is a crucial difference between inserting Asian Pacific Americans into the American story as it has been told and retelling the American story in the voices that have not been heard. The difference reveals what those voices will say. Roksana Badruddoja's *National (Un)Belonging: Bengali American Women on Imagining and Contesting Culture and Identity* is a compelling illustration of why this difference matters. *National (Un)Belonging* reveals a multilay-ered and sophisticated portrait of South Asian American identity. Her study reminds readers that contemporary identity is always interwoven with class, culture, diaspora, family, gender, race, sexuality, and spirituality in complex ways with ever-shifting degrees of consequence. Badruddoja suggests that identity is rarely a settled or simple definition. Her subjects disclose many important details about how being a South Asian American woman is equally limiting, liberating, political, and benign. Badruddoja's commitment to pro-gressive and interdisciplinary research methods enriches the work of telling America's whole story. Indeed, the study of a changing, pluralistic American society requires innovative and multifaceted forms of scholarly inquiry; these American voices are revealing and worth hearing. For Asian Pacific Americans, *National (Un)Belonging* will be familiar in how it captures the cultural calculus behind our experience.

I am touched by how Badruddoja views her work as a personal journey. I find this to be the case for many Asian American studies scholars; our work is always personal. Given that our history, art, and culture have often been told through other voices—if at all—there are few role models from which to draw direction during moments when we want it. The Smithsonian Asian Pacific American Program remains committed to offering answers to the ques-tion of what the voices of Asian Pacific American history, art, and culture have to say. Previous exhibitions by the Program suggest how Japanese American identity is tied to the internment; or how Filipino American identity is tied to colonialism; or Vietnamese American identity is tied to the Vietnam War; or how Indian American identity is tied to incidents in the wake of September 11, 2001. But in the absence of fully realized version of Asian Pacific American history being represented in national institutions such as the Smithsonian in ways similar to America's other communities, our scholarship and work will

remain personal: we are creating a canon so that our children and later generations may be able to find guidance or points of contestation in telling the Asian
Pacific American story.

Konrad Ng

CHAPTER 1

The Cheshire Cat
Vexing Identities

In November 2004, on an unusually warm weekday afternoon, I found myself
ushering Rupa into my mother's suburban home in Burr Ridge, Illinois—one
of my interview sites. Our interview began in my mom's efficient home office,
and after more than three hours of speaking to each other, Rupa and I desperately needed a small break to nurture our depleted minds and bodies. We
shared a steaming bowl of matter paneer and naan, a meal my mom prepared
that morning and left for us on her large cherry wood kitchen table. In between
silence and bites of our meal, Rupa lifted her head and said to me,

> I was born here [the United States], but there is part of me that feels like
> I don't belong here. I don't have that draw; that pull it is not the same ...
> I currently embody everything that the majority of, at least eligible, vot-
> ers hate. I am queer, Muslim, and brown. What else is there?

> Of course, I come back to my senses ... The last time I went to Bangladesh
> was seven years ago ... There is an air about the way I walk or the way
> I talk, even when I am speaking Bengali. Someone even said eye contact
> marks me a little different, so I am Othered in that way [too].

In a single moment, during our "off" time, Rupa demonstrated how she volleys
between the perceived tension between Americanness and South Asianness
and dialogues with national (un)belonging. The global pandemic has placed
large and pressing questions around the relationship between the extant systems of nationhood, border control, the nation-state, and the mass movement
of diasporic populations. Rupa's words put into motion a pertinent theme in
this book: She insightfully problematizes the clash of cultures and civilizations
discourse (the Orientalist east/west divide) and the binary categorization
between South Asian and American and she challenges the debates around
race, ethnicity, gender, sexuality, class, religion, culture, youth, and citizenship.

The research on which this book is based explores the meanings of national
belonging and unbelonging for a group of second-generation South Asian
women in America. In this work, I focus on the multiple discursive geopolitical positioning staged by the now adult children of post-1965 immigrants

from "South Asia". I explore the perceptions of second-generation South Asian, namely Bengali, American women about daily social practices in the U.S. and how they view themselves in comparison to broader American society. I do this by engaging in a year-long feminist ethnography in 2004, with a cross-national sample of twenty-five women in the U.S. I spent a day in the life of each woman, eating and drinking and talking about work, partners, families, food, clothing, and how they feel about being children of immigrants.

To encourage the ongoing process of interdisciplinary imagination, dialogue, critique, and revisions, I confront how individuals make sense of and handle multiple and conflicting identities (Dhingra 2007, 1) by asking the following questions: What are the meanings of ABCD or American-Born Confused Desi—a popular term for second-generation South Asian Americans—in the U.S. racial and ethnic imaginary ("desi" derives from the Hindi word "desh," meaning motherland; "desi" is a diasporic identity term used by South Asians to refer to being South Asian)? How do these meanings travel through class, gender, sexual, and cultural hierarchies both in the United States and transnationally? By asking such questions, I focus on both the conceptual and theoretical perspectives of the social, economic, cultural, aesthetic, and political dimensions of transnational migration, which includes the effects of population circulations and demographic change (community formation, segregation, and integration).

What I find through my original ethnographic data is that national (un)belonging plays a critical role in the ways in which second-generation Bengali American women imagine their identities. While Rupa's sense of social differentiation is a product of dominant discourses of white supremacy (and male privilege and heteronormativity), and the women with whom I worked locate themselves in a series of binaries (to express social differentiation), the general category of Other, though relevant, does not work on its own. American Orientalism (à la Said) as a framework does not wholly explain the complex lives my participants lead.[1] Dhingra (2007) offers the second-generation "have

---

1   American Orientalism incorporates a socially constructed division of the world into two distinct and mutually exclusive categories with hierarchical features attached to each side, one that empowers "whiteness" (and maleness and heterosexuality) and marginalizes non-whites (and femaleness and non-heterosexuality) (Fanon 1986; McIntosh 1988; Puar and Rai 2002). The Orient is codified as poor, unfree, and ahistorical, marking the Asian as undynamic and placing Asia under Eurocentric rule and gaze (Prashad 2000, 12). The Orient is also imagined as feminine—passive, spiritual, and traditional, and in contrast, the Occident is frequently configured as masculine—aggressive, rational, and modern (Yoshihara 2003). Yet, within Orientalist traditions, the sexual norms of the Orient, such as the "Middle East,"

multiple identities that they define as both in tension and as in dialogue" (9). My respondents articulate their identities at the intersections of a constellation of loyalties that are multiple, contradictory, constantly shifting, and overlapping. The women in this study rupture Mohanty's (1988) theoretical "Third World Woman" and adopt Dhingra's (2007) notion of "lived hybridity." And, throughout the ethnographic research, the theme of sexuality—South Asian daughterhood—circumscribes the ways my research participants imagine and contest culture, identity, and belonging (Naber 2006, 87–88). I uncover a secret: The women in my fieldwork articulate a complex process in which the categories "South Asian" and "American" are mutually constitutive and exist both as opposites and in unison, representing Naber's (2006) "selective assimilation strategy" (88).

The conceptual insights gained from studying second-generation South Asian American women are not limited. The strategic emergence involves the transformation of critical dimensions, such as culture, ancestral family relationships, sexuality, religion, and communal belonging to a nation. National (un)belonging is subject to a heavily contested debate, and, through my interviews, I determined identity is the issue that best captures the class of events. A central theme that emerged from the data is how my respondents "perform"—experience—their identities as "South Asian American" women. The women's stories underscore the agency individuals have in asserting, enhancing, maintaining, and reconstructing their identities. I focus on broader theoretical and epistemological concerns—identity, identity grammar, and shifts in identity grammar (Brekhus 2003)—within the context of national (un)belonging. And I situate the study on the margins of both racialized U.S. nationalism and South Asian American cultural nationalism, within intersecting coordinates of power—race, ethnicity, class, gender, sexuality, and nation. The identity transformations of the women involved in my fieldwork may have considerable impact on social behavior in a wide range of contexts, including economic life and political democracy. One of the objectives of the book, then, is to make progress on the understanding of issues surrounding the nation-state and population circulations and demographic change by shedding light on some current developments and practical responses by second-generation Bengali American women. This book illuminates the paradoxes of national belonging, exclusion, alienation, and political expression for a generation of Bengali

---

are interpreted as paradoxically repressed and perverse—the Orient is "the site of carefully suppressed animalistic sexual instincts" (Puar 2004, 526). The occidental constructions of the Orient, then, tend to posit the "east" as the polar and frequently inferior opposite of the "west" (Said 1979): The "east" is static and unfree, and the "west" is dynamic and free.

American women, and it also sheds light on larger questions of globalization and for those concerned with the role of the United States in the world today.

1   Experience/Theory

My academic endeavors stem from my autobiographical history (Spivak 1988; hooks 1990; Puar 1994a, Puar 1994b). Puar's (1994a) experience/theory divide, within which this book is situated, is invaluable:

> I ... believe that the relationships between experience and theory are contingent, discontinuous, and contradictory ... Just as readers are situated in multiple discursive geopolitical positionings, I too, as an author, can situate and resituate myself and thus my text as reflective of my selves. (78)

Therefore, like Narayan (1997), "I ... wish to suggest some linkages between the complexities of who I am and what I claim to know" (5). I take a moment to clarify my influences.

As a child and adolescent in the 1970s and 80s, I juggled and moved between my "South Asian" identity and my "American" identity, which at times felt distinct to me. I remember a daily two-step ritual after coming home from elementary school (in Elgin, Illinois) that would transform me from an "American" to a "South Asian" (Bangladeshi) girl and daughter. First, before entering my home, I take off my sneakers—my outside shoes—in the garage and slip into my *bashar jootha*, or indoor sandals. Next, I shed my ESPRIT outfit, take a shower, and slip into a silk *shalwar kameez*. The purification act, which consisted of a simple procedure of shedding, cleansing, and changing, cognitively switched from a world of "American" friendship bracelets to one of "South Asian" gold bangles. As an adult, I separate my desi clothing from my "American" clothes in my closet.[2] I use space and time for the purposes of segregation (Nippert-Eng 1995/1996). Implicit in the segregation is the idea of (symbolic) pollution (Douglas 2001).[3]

---

2 Such "polarization" or "mental fencing" is characteristic of boundary-work (mutual exclusivity), and it is a way in which individuals (or organizations) can simplify and order their environment (Zerubavel 1991).

3 Pollution, uncleanness, or dirt is that which must not be included if a pattern is to be maintained. It breaches classifications and is anomalous or ambiguous (Douglas 2001, 2).

The categories that I understand myself to belong to and the ways in which others see me carry social meaning. Power clusters around certain categories while exercising against others (Sandoval 1982; Mohanty 1988; Anzaldúa 2001). I am often asked where my homeland is, where I learned to speak English well (without an accent or an American accent), and when I "arrived" in this country. When gender is highlighted, I receive questions such as, "Was your marriage arranged?" Yet, as I strategically decode my identity with binary language—"South Asian" versus "American"—I am forced to confront the idea of an imagined "true" South Asian culture and a heterogeneous South Asian culture in the context of migration, assimilation, and racialization. I can recall several experiences growing up within a bicultural Bengali American familial and communal context: *Amerikan ra* (Americans are) trash and immoral and *Bangali ra* (Bengalis are) invested in family values and hospitality (Naber 2006, 87). At "Bengali" parties, I am a "respectable South Asian woman" through dress, language, and behavior—the "desi virgin." I am in opposition to the average American woman—the "American(ized) whore" (Naber 2006, 88). The goal is to convey to the community that, despite being raised in the United States, my parents protected me from the "corrupt 'west'." I am an imagined "true" South Asian woman. My parents make clear the cultural expectations they have of me as a South Asian American daughter, though they eagerly highlight that I am different from my cousins "back home" in Bangladesh: I am an American, and, therefore, "different (read as "better" and "privileged"). The "dirty little secret" is the South Asian Diaspora is vested in a selective assimilation strategy in which the preservation of South Asian cultural identity and assimilation to American norms of whiteness are simultaneously desired (Naber 2006). Indeed, the ways in which individuals "do" their identities is constrained or facilitated by forces outside their social control (Jones 2001, 7).

The theme of female sexuality circumscribes the ways culture, identity, and belonging are imagined and contested (Naber 2006, 88) and is central to the discussion and framework of the book. The ontology begins to rearticulate the ongoing debates about race, ethnicity, sexuality, and gender in relation to nationhood and I am prompted to think about the Orientalist "Third World Woman" trope versus real women who have multiple and contradictory alliances (Mohanty 1988). Race and gender debates highlight the very real problems posed by "western" feminist discourse, the ground in which Mohanty (1988) pivots her work on the relationship between Woman—a cultural and ideological composite Other constructed through diverse representational discourse—and women—real, material subjects and their collective herstories. Mohanty underscores one of the central trepidations against feminist scholarship in America: The discursive colonization of the material and historical heterogeneities of the lives of "global south" women. In November 2001, Laura Bush, in her radio address to the nation in support of the war in Iraq, deployed essentialized "east/west" imagery to offer a discourse of salvation, advocating the necessity, responsibility, duty, and the God-given right of America to save trapped (and backward) Muslim women from the practice of purdah (Abu-Lughod 2003). I continue to be dumbfounded by publications in popular mass-media magazines with titles like "Terrorized for being smart, young and female." In a June 2005 issue of *Glamour*, I find the following passage: "Since early 2004 dozens of young female Iraqis have been targeted and executed by extremist Islamic insurgents ... all because they dared to be modern women ... One woman once told me that before she would wear a veil, she'd cut her head off ..." (136). It would be a mistake to view these events as simply reactions to infringement of democratic ideals. Purdah is a cultural practice that, in and of itself, may not raise questions of power and difference. When inserted into the hiatus between the "east" and the "west," the practice of veiling or seclusion is part of an untroubled model of secular progressivism in which the veil can be read as only a trope of incarceration (Mohanty 1988). When "culture" is read from brown women's bodies in such ways, gender is conflated with ideas and feelings about race, ethnicity, and the nation (Narayan 1997; Nagel 2003).

Such category work informs collective and individual experiences and identities of not only migrants and their children in America but also of hegemonic Americans. Because of discursive colonization, I was not "American" enough in elementary school and I was too "western" or "corrupt" for my immigrant parents (Maira 2002, 4). Hasnat's (1998) essay "Being 'Amreekan': Fried Chicken versus Chicken Tikka" haunted me. Like the Cheshire Cat in Lewis Carroll's *Alice's Adventures in Wonderland* (1865), I felt I had no sense of self at times. The composite single Third World Woman carries in the American imaginations the authorizing signature of "western" humanistic discourse, effacing the possibility that women of color may be vested in both "their" cultural identity and racialized American subjectivities. In this study, the twenty-five women's biographies clarify my own notions of my identity, guiding me toward a project of self-recovery and reconciliation with myself. The women taught me that I do not have one identity; rather, I can identify on many grounds—across race, class, gender, nationality, sexuality, etc.—in simultaneous and contradictory ways, and they do not operate with equal importance in all situations. What began as feelings of isolation and the need for separation ended with a personal project of identity—a process of "front-staging" and "back-staging" of identity categories (Collins 2004) with multidimensional histories.

2   Theoretical and Methodological Implications

Binary constructs within "white, western, and feminist thinking" (Puar 1993) provide an important conceptual tool through which I can evaluate the women's stories that are at the center of my research. The oppositional poles of east/west, white/Black, man/woman, and South Asian/American acquire social significance and meaning through Said's (1979) Orientalist knowledge production—an assumed experience based on dominant representation—rendering the second-generation as misplaced and cultural conflict-bound (Puar 1994a, 23). The construction and maintenance of an oppositional South Asian that is mutually exclusive of the white American is facilitated by the reluctance of the dominant "white gazes" or "trope of the racialized gaze" (Fanon 1986) to acknowledge some form of interdependence on the other. My research participants believe social differentiation to be a product of dominant discourses of white, male, and heterosexual privileges. Kelly (1998) illustrates the complex meanings attached to the "white gaze," and one that allows a dominant group to control the social spaces and social interaction of all groups and subdues those who receive it and make them wish to be invisible (19). The "white gaze" does not suggest that whiteness is monolithic, devoid of multiple ideologies and configurations, but rather, I refer to the insistence of oppositional boundaries clearly marked and upheld as mutually exclusive realities that mythologize a cohesive white identity (Puar 1994a, 23). Consider the "model-minority" myth. First, it elides the existence of refugees, undocumented workers, and working-class immigrants, imbuing South Asian communities with a false homogeneity (Zhou 1997; Prashad 2000; Ngai 2004; Kwong and Miščević 2005). Second, it reproduces the idea of Asian American foreignness, thus denying sameness vis-à-vis white society and preventing drawing parallels across class and gender (Puar 1994a, 23). Puar (1994a) argues that the either/or equation freezes the South Asian Other without political or social agency or room to negotiate subjectivity, maintaining the focus on exclusionary politics by marginalizing those with multiple alliances (24–25).

The women I interviewed align themselves with American nationalism (often along class lines), while also distancing themselves from their Americanness through racial, ethnic, and cultural definitions (Puar 1993; Prashad 2000, 2002, 2003). Much like Dhingra's (2007) respondents who suggest the multifaceted nature of how people maintain multiple commitments, the women's self-definitions include manipulation and expressions of opposition as they grew to appreciate "their culture" while simultaneously owning being American. Puar (1994a) calls this strategy "bargaining with racism" and "oppositionally active whiteness." She writes:

Such a notion of identity suggests a complete alliance with neither South Asian nor white society; rather, it resists both. It is opposition in its unwillingness to be consumed by the white pole; activity in this arena results not from racism or rejection by white society. It is instead the product of critical evaluation and appreciation of one's own culture. (27)

M respondents develop a "reactive ethnicity" (Dhingra's 2007, 5) and do not ignore colonial histories and often boldly challenge Orientalist conquest. The women (consciously and unconsciously) respond to oppression and manipulate hooks' (1992) "terror of whiteness" (Puar 1994a), constructing "resistant identities" and articulating an "oppositional consciousness" (Sandoval 1991, Panjabi 1997).[4] At the same time, while the women align themselves with South Asianness, they also oppositionally implicate themselves with freedom, individuality, and falling in love as "western"/American cultural ideals. The desire of stereotypical "Americanness" is predicated on "South Asianness" as the crucial Other (Naber 2006). Dhingra (2007) brings focus to the issue here:

So much of the discourse on ethnicity ... refers to American culture as modern and as prioritizing the individual relative to a traditional and constraining immigrant heritage. This discursive dichotomy conceals the cultural conservatisms found in America, including the constraints placed on women and the rise of overt religiosity. Yet Asian Americans themselves often interpret their experiences within this framework. (2–3)

My point is, while the informants challenge the east/west dichotomy and marks themselves as a racial and cultural Other, exhibiting their loyalties to South Asianness, they also underscore their alliance to U.S. nationalist culture. Visweswaran (1993) expresses the nature of second-generation identities by pointing to an "oscillation between post-colonial and racialized American subjectivities" (309). The women show, in the context of immigration, assimilation, and racialization, "South Asian" and "American" exist as both opposites and in unison—a persisting and central theme in the study. The Orientalist east/west and tradition/modernity dichotomies fall far behind the actual construction of the women's identities and dispersion of culture.

Immigration scholars, like Portes and Rumbaut, point to the fundamentals of multiculturalism. They articulate a one-dimension identity model with

---

4 One does not have to consciously negotiate/reject/appropriate/manage identity to be an agent (Freeman 2000).

assimilation on one side and whiteness as the benchmark, and ethnic enclaves on the other side—discrete and divided ethnic and racial communities. I find the question is not about assimilation, ethnic enclaves, or anything in between. My research participants collapse the one-dimensional multicultural model by producing multiple identities simultaneously, validating the categories that define human visibility as well as invisibility in public spaces. They struggle to fashion a space for themselves outside of this multicultural identity model. The women break apart and reject models of assimilation along with ethnic enclave identity models. One of the methodological insights then is the hazards of definition and power play that is behind any attempt to box a living, breathing, and fragmented thinker. Therefore, my primary goal is to allow the twenty-five women I interviewed to speak about their (auto)biographical experiences and be heard and represented through the book.[5] Second, I wish to frame the experiences of the women within "objective" data processes, scientific analysis, and sociological and feminist theory. In this light, I do not claim that the twenty-five women's words are representative of the second-generation South Asian American community at large or that they are even representative of themselves. The category "South Asian" is heterogeneous and must be deconstructed. The phenomenon of intersectionality cannot be generalized as taking on one singular form for all second-generation South Asian American women; we must be cautious using the terms "South Asian," "South Asian American," and "South Asian American woman" (Islam 1993; Mani 1993; Visweswaran 1993; Puar 1994a; Poore 1998). Naber (2006) argues feminist theory and practice "should take the specific ways that the coordinates of race, class, gender, sexuality, religion, and nation intersect in different contexts seriously" (91). Hence, the book is not an analysis of all second-generation South Asian American women. I use the words of the women with whom I worked to speak for myself and to facilitate my understanding of the women's lives, to think beyond misperceptions and stereotypes, and to make comments about the larger theme of identity, which best describes the class of events in this study. An interdisciplinary methodological stance was necessary to invoke the multiply layered and contradictory experiences. And it is precisely because I employ a host of methods from various disciplines, e.g., comparative historical and feminist approaches, that I can break down and deconstruct binaries, concluding that no model of identity will suffice to explain the experiences of

---

5 While, I have edited my respondents' words into a readable form, including cutting repetitive words, rearranging the order of the narratives, and simplifying elaborate explanations (Naber 2006), I maintain the originality of the women's words as much as possible.

the twenty-five second-generation Bengali American women who took part in this study.

3   Under-heard and Under-theorized Identities

I concentrate on women because when emphasizing the opposition of men and women, the woman is the marked Other (Yegenoglu 1998), and masculinity is the unmarked or the normal (Connell 1995). When men become the marked, such as Arab American men, women do not become the unmarked, but, rather, they disappear (Brooks 2004).[6] Consistently, there is a hierarchical margin between men and women. Within this gender juxtaposition, the social treatment of women is problematic at best and deadly at worst around the world and has taken on an added dimension in the South Asian American context. Like Samina Ali's protagonist Layla in *Madras on Rainy Days*, adult daughters have been taken to South Asia and married to prevent cultural and racial contamination (Dasgupta and Warrier 1997). Mohanty (1993) argues the construction of femininity and masculinity, especially in relation to the idea of the nation, are central to fundamentalist rhetoric and mobilization. She writes, "Religious fundamentalist constructions of women embody the nexus of morality, sexuality and Nation ... Women are not only mobilized in the 'service' of the Nation, but they also become the ground on which the discourse of morality and nationalism are written" (356). South Asian daughters are responsible for maintaining family honor and culture (while sons have the obligation of caring for their parents in their old age.) A daughter's husband is a benchmark for her own personal success and the family (Dasgupta and Warrier 1997; Shah 1997; Dasgupta 1989). A daughter's procreational obligation goes beyond her own life, stretching out into society's expectations and far ahead into future generations in the name of cultural preservation. The ideal of reproducing cultural identity, then, is gendered and sexualized and disproportionately placed on daughters (cross-culturally and cross-nationally). A daughter's rejection of an idealized notion of South Asian womanhood signifies cultural loss, negating her potential as capital within this family strategy (Naber 2006, 88). I find in this study the women's role in their communities is that of being "carriers of culture," and the ideal of reproducing culture is highly gendered and differentially associated with women (Narayan 2000). Women, particularly women of

---

6 Media focus on same sex acts of torture of male Iraqi prisoners at Abu Ghraib obscures other forms of gendered violence and serves a broader racist, sexist, and homophobic agenda (Puar 2004, 522–23).

color, are constantly and commonly constructed as the marked Other, where Othering is a practice of domination (Mohanty 1988; Sandoval 1991; Byrne 2000a, Byrne 2000b; Anzaldúa 2001). As a category, women of color are often under-theorized (Yegenoglu 1998).

I focus on South Asians because even though they are a relatively newly arrived "ethnic" group and they are one of the fastest-growing groups in the United States. Past decades have seen massive population movements of South Asians—mostly Indians, Pakistanis, and Bangladeshis—from South Asia to the United States. An influx of South Asian migration began after the Immigration and Naturalization Act of 1965.[7] The South Asian community expanded from 50,000 before 1965 to 815,000 by 1990, and by 2000 had reached 1,687,765 (Hing 1993). However, South Asians, especially women, are one of the most "underserved" immigrant communities in the United States. Even though government and public policies place community and social services as a priority on their agendas, this attention has not been focused equally on all communities. To a large extent, immigrant communities in America have escaped "social watchfulness" and suffer from a lack of services and resources. The South Asian community critically suffers from this oversight. The lack of social watchfulness is in part due to the dearth of research on social problems affecting the South Asian American community. Due to the paucity of research, there are little reliable statistical data on the incidence rate of gender-specific abuse in the South Asian American community, leading to the widespread belief that gender-based violence (e.g., spousal abuse) is not a serious problem among South Asians in America (the myth of the model-minority) (Dasgupta and Warrier 1997). As a result of COVID-19, domestic violence calls from South Asian American immigrant women to South Asian American domestic violence organizations—like *Manavi, Sakhi, Maitri,* and *Narika*—abruptly halted soon after March 12, 2020 (Kam 2020). Women with abusive partners found themselves unable to connect with domestic violence advocates they were working with before the pandemic because women were trapped at home with their abusers. Mukherji (2020) documents how women struggled to make phone calls with their abusers at home, e.g., "One woman hid in her closet to make the call." The silence was chilling for two months and as the "lockdowns" eased in May and June 2020, organizations experienced a surge in calls as a response to the increase in abuse during the pandemic (Kam 2020). Additionally, in the wake of the global pandemic, South Asian

---

7 In October of 1965, amendments to the 1952 Immigration and Nationality Act repealed the national origins quota system (Ngai 2004).

groups are targets of violent racist attacks, while administrations give rise to ethnocentric government programs such as the U.S. Visitor and Immigrant Status Indicator Technology, calling into question who is an American and who is not.

4   Contribution to the Literature

The continued influx of South Asian immigrants raises several scholarly questions, such as what changes occur in South Asian immigrant families when they move to the United States, which a growing number of researchers have addressed (Fisher 1980; Gibson 1988; Agarwal 1991; Lessinger 1995; Mukhi 2000). However, less visible in the media and scholarship are the children of these immigrants. The offspring of post-1965 immigrants began to come of age during the late 1980s and 1990s, but the stories of these South Asian Americans have not yet adequately been told and incorporated into the larger narratives of the United States (Maira 2002, 2). Narratives of gender are often based on the white, middle-class, female experience, while the narratives of race are based often on the black male experience (Crenshaw 1991). Nationality and citizenship discussions produce an epistemological discourse that centers on white, heterosexual, and generally male histories (Waters 1990; Brodkin 1998; Ignatiev 1995; Guglielmo 2003). There is an urgent need to account for multiple grounds of identity when considering how the social world is constructed (Crenshaw 1991; Mohanty 2003, 244). Hence, in this research, I illuminate the process of identity work from the voices of second-generation Bengali American women. The children of these immigrants represent a critical generation, determining patterns of race, ethnicity, culture, economy, and politics in the United States. Maira (2002) writes, "Immigrant youth culture raises questions about the relationships of immigrant communities to the nation-state in which they live and the one they ostensibly left behind" (21). A central question, therefore, is what kinds of identities are second-generation South Asian Americans forging?

This book is sociologically significant because I examine perceptions and daily social practices. Earlier studies on South Asian populations (Fisher 1980; Gibson 1988; Agarwal 1991; Lessinger 1995; Mukhi 2000) have not paid sufficient attention to the way members of that population view themselves in comparison to broader American society. The literature on the second-generation frequently underscores the process by which they are adjusting to American society (Prashad 2000; Maira 2002; Purkayastha 2005). Two main theoretical perspectives—assimilation (Portes and Rumbaut 2001) and pluralism

(Conzen 1991)—commonly have been the basis for examining that adjustment process. Central to the assimilation perspective is the assumption that there is a natural process by which diverse ethnic groups come to share a common culture and gain equal access to opportunities (Gordon 1964). Alternatively, the pluralist perspective perceives American society as consisting of a harmonious collection of culturally distinct ethnic and racial groups (Zhou 1997). I am concerned with the aspect of social life that the two perspectives tend to downplay. While the perspectives are often characterized as different, they have two features in common that have not yet been sufficiently transcended. In both instances, the research on second-generation populations focuses on outcome: On the one hand, the result is assimilation, and on the other hand, it is a form of power sharing. Beyond their emphasis on outcome, however, both positions are fundamentally focused on the extent to which those outcomes serve to diminish social conflict within society. The "outcome" focus can then be seen as oriented toward the absorptive ability of the social system as a whole. The ability of the social system to adapt to diverse populations is a valuable research agenda. However, it does not provide an understanding of the equally valuable research concern with the inner workings of the individuals. Grewal (1994) writes, "The debates on assimilation and nonassimilation might elide the important projects of complicity with and utilization of difference ..." (53). This study indicates that second-generation individuals are engaged in the complicated process of simultaneously mediating a multitude of racialized national cultures. As such, a new set of social circumstances came into the first decade of the twenty-first century, and it, in turn, provided a fresh set of cultural phenomena for those engaging in society.

This book is about how second-generation South Asian, namely Bengali, American women make sense of their everyday relationship to the State by interrogating their daily identity-making practices and everyday discursive experiences. The issue of "cultural belonging" is a critical one, for it goes to the heart of experiences of community belonging and exclusion. Here, I challenge how the identities and experiences of second-generation South Asian American women are imagined in the mass media and in public discourse. Following in the footsteps of Naber (2006), this study argues for an anti-essentialist approach to Asian American Studies that take historical and localized conditions seriously (and there is a growing need for academic departments to become increasingly integrated to better understand the world's political, social, and economic issues that hegemonically maintain the cultural and economic hierarchy.) Thus, I consider my subjects to be more than second-generation South Asian American women, presenting them also as individual cultural producers and consumers strengthening the American nation-state.

What I offer in the book is a conception of difference not as a fixed category but as certain relation, and a new (imaginary) hierarchy of difference. I address the experiences of the South Asian Diaspora by conceptualizing difference and highlighting how marginality is a powerful space in which culture is produced and consumed daily. In today's world of globalization, neoliberal capitalism is based on exploitation of spatial and cultural differences, and there are multiple hierarchies in the everyday practices of differentiation and the construction of Otherness (Jain 2005; Brooks 2007). I am suggesting that clear binary differences disappear. This study presents the narratives of race, ethnicity, color, gender, nationality, and citizenship from the (auto)biographical recounts of twenty-five second-generation Bengali American women, and my goal is to get beyond stories of assimilation and generational conflict, producing a more nuanced construction of identity and the self.

5   Contesting Unitary Self

Moving forward, in Chapter 2, I seek to review the body of contemporary im/migration literature on South Asian Americans and their children—the second-generation. I work to develop a historical framework in which to contextualize how the twenty-five second-generation Bengali American women in this study perceive and engage in daily social practices in the United States and how they view themselves in comparison to broader American society. In Chapter 3, I explore methodology, feminist approaches, and research implications. This chapter examines the process of my research from the point of imagining the study to completion. I outline how I begin to approach my research process. Here, I not only interrogate knowledge production as a researcher, but I also contemplate what the women's stories suggest methodologically. Next, racial and ethnic projects have an enormous effect on the production of space, and the process of producing space has an enormous effect on subject formation (Simmel 1950; Brady 2002).

In Chapter 4, I probe the ways in which South Asians in America are racialized and the ways in which they respond to U.S. racial projects, including how the women in this study use racial and ethnic labels. I find that the women sort themselves by contesting notions of race—"Asian"—and appropriating ethnic discourse—"Bengali" and "South Asian." However, their refusal to identify solely as racial subjects ("ethnicity paradigm") does not mean they wholly reject the existence of race, nor does it mean that they get to absolve themselves from racial categorization. In Chapter 5, I discuss the meanings of "culture" and "cultural identity" through the eyes of the women in this study.

I find that while the women I interviewed express the theme of culture within binaries, positioning South Asianness in strict opposition to Americanness, they simultaneously engage in assimilatory acts, protecting the boundaries of U.S. nationalism and hegemonic discourse, which is predicated on delineating South Asian from American through Orientalism and Otherness. In this discussion, my research participants' distinction between being "South Asian" and "American" often break down, suggesting that the South Asian community is not altogether a different conception of spatiality.

In Chapter 6, I present five discursive sites—language, holidays, religion, cooking and eating, and clothing—that my research participants collectively identify as spaces of cathexis in which they produce and consume culture daily. I call the five sites "territories of the self." My respondents suggest that they (re-)negotiate their identity performances continually and consistently through the five discursive sites of cultural production. Meaning, the women I interviewed reject hegemonic conceptions of a unitary self. In Chapter 7, I extend on Third Wave literature, which often ignores the subject of "home." I accomplish this by including the social and geographical constructions of home: What is it? And where is it? In this chapter, I address assimilationist configurations of the questions "What is home?" and "Where are you from?" The Other narrative is legitimized and enforced by "Where are you *really* from?" The question is exclusionary and racist. Here, "home" is embedded in a linear construction of place, which is situated, fixed, and safe. Chapter 7 serves to challenge assimilationist configurations and linear constructions of "home," what it means, and where it is.

In Chapter 8, I focus on the role marriage plays in my research participants' lives. I explore how the women in this study respond to their families' expectations of marriage along with the women's own expectations of marriage within the context of hegemonic U.S. nationalism, pressures of assimilation, gendered racialization of South Asian women, and localized imagined "true" South Asian culture. I find that heterosexual ethno-religious endogamous marriage is a key demand of South Asian American womanhood. In Chapter 9, I continue to develop the concept of identity-work—the complexity of my informants' identity and the idea that identity involves not just experience but also actual practices—by focusing on queer-identified second-generation Bengali Americans. I share two of my respondents' stories: Rupa and Ronica. I extend scholarship on the South Asian Diaspora by underscoring areas of weakness in queer theory and in literature about migration/ U.S. identity formation.

In Chapter 10, I review popular, award-winning South Asian diasporic novels and I use the literary fictions as sites of possible ruptures in lived experiences of second-generation Bengali American women. As I sociologically probe the dispersion of cultural experiences through the literary fictional narratives and compare them across situations within a set of lives in my ethnographic work, the identity formations portrayed in popular fictions seem untenable. Too often, popular literary fictions spawned by South Asian diasporic authors for consumption by both the diaspora and "western" (often read as "white") mainstream are laden with Orientalist dualities. Finally, in Chapter 11, I discuss the sociological lessons l earned: The theme of identity and shifting identity best captures the class of events described in this research. Here, I challenge a rigid socio-cognitive framework, or the inability to break away from com-partmentalizing bodies, by reading bodies in multiple ways. I offer solutions to rigid-identity work.

In sum, the book goes beyond the question of identity for South Asians who are born and/or raised in America. My research participants' oral histories speak to the gendered and sexualized discourses of assimilation, racism, and U.S. Orientalism, as well as the multiple points in which they break down. I focus on community formation, segregation, and integration, and what I uncover is that national (un)belonging plays a critical role in the ways in which second-generation South Asian American women imagine their identities. Hence, I situate my research on the margins of both U.S. racialized nationalism and South Asian cultural nationalism. This book contributes to a better understanding of im/migration studies; intersectional studies; comparative racial and ethnic structures; nationhood, nationality, and citizenship; colonial and postcolonial studies; gender and women's studies; feminist and queer theory; sociology of the self; and South Asian and urban American studies. It will be of interest to scholars, social critics, and general readers whose commitment lie in tracking the relationship between the American nation-state and the movement of human populations across national borders.

CHAPTER 2

Impossible Subjects

(Re)Collecting South Asian American Im/migration

In this chapter, I concentrate on literature about contemporary South Asian American immigrant communities and second-generation youth communities. The history of arrival helps to clarify the racial projects immigrants are inserted into, and subsequently the ways in which they see themselves within American racial structures. My goal is to draw upon earlier works to develop a historical framework for contextualizing how the twenty-five second-generation Bengali American women in this study perceive and engage in daily social practices in the United States and how they view themselves in comparison to broader American society. I clarify the link between the normative power of discourse and the history of marginalized groups in America.

1   Welcome Desis ... Not!: 1965 to 1990

In 1965, U.S. law revised the half-century-old policy that barred Asian immigrants from entering the country. USSR's Sputnik I and II launches in the late 1950s threw the United States into panic. The development of U.S. science relied heavily on immigrants from the 1940s, such as Albert Einstein and Enrico Fermi, and in their desire to compete with the "eastern" bloc's technological advancements, the U.S. government promoted the study of science and technology through a better-funded National Science Foundation and by local projects such as the "math bees." America launched an international search for natural scientists who could promote U.S. scientific study along with medical personnel to fill the increased demand for doctors due to the legislated Medicare and Medicaid programs. On July 23, 1963, President Kennedy informed the legislature that he wanted to see the immigration system overhauled so that "highly trained or skilled persons may obtain a preference without requiring that they secure employment here before emigrating" (Prashad 2000, 74). The Immigration Act of 1965 was a watershed legislation of the Kennedy-Johnson era. The amendments represented one of the most important revisions of immigration policy in the United States since the First Quota Act of 1921. Under the old Immigration and Nationality Act of 1952, officials allowed a certain percentage of the total number of immigrants from a given nation already residing in the United States. In lieu of the considerations of nationality and ethnicity, the 1965 amendments established a quota system based on nation-state, reunification of families, and needed skills; the amendments granted individual visas with priority given to these criteria as well as refugee status (Ngai 2004). Since 1965, sources of im/migration to the United States shifted from Europe to Asia and other parts of the "developing" world.

The new law had profound effects on the "third world," creating greater "opportunities" for migration from Asia in particular. The 1965 act made the annual maximum quota of "Eastern Hemisphere" immigrants 170,000 and no more than 20,000 per country. Throughout U.S. history, im/migrant workers have been used as docile and cheap manual labor and technical workers and the bulk of South Asian migration before 1965 contained the latter.

The revised law shifted to "highly qualified" South Asian (mostly Indian) technical workers who quickly establishing themselves in the United States as highly educated, middle- to upper-middle-class skilled professionals (Agarwal 1991). Ngai (2004) writes, "[The] signal achievement [of the 1965 Act] was that it ended the policy of admitting immigrants according to a hierarchy of racial desirability and established the principle of formal equality in immigration" (227), increasing the possibility of migration opportunities from Asia (and eastern and southern Europe, the object of exclusion in the Immigration Act of 1924). As such, the Immigration Act of 1965 "has been canonized in history and social sciences as the apotheosis of postwar liberalism, cultural pluralism, and democratic mobilization ..." (Ngai 2004, 227).

The birth narrative of the 1965 Act implies a national recognition that America is composed of diversity of ethno-racial groups and growing political support for cultural pluralism. But the law was not about equality. Despite the liberal inclusionary narrative, the Immigration Act of 1965 is composed of exclusionary features modeling a developmentalist nation-state discourse. Lawmakers' intent was to continue preferential treatment of white immigrant entry by replacing racial language with language of family reunification: white immigrant would bring their relatives. Here, the 1965 law introduced H-1B visas—temporary, high-skilled work permits—and there was no expectation that the technical category migrants who later naturalized would use their citizenship to bring their families into the United States. To be clear, lawmakers did not count on "global south" immigrant to use family reunification to the degree that they did. When immigration reformers spoke of "rights," they referred to the rights of existing Americans—the ethnic Euro-Americans— and not the rights of migrants (Ngai 2004). Ngai (2004) expresses, "The Hart-Celler Act furthered the trend of the 1920s that placed questions of territoriality, border control, and abstract categories of status at the center of

immigration law" (264). The question of citizenship was an amorphous variable in immigration policy and reform discourse. Alongside the "liberalization"
of quota as assigned to the eastern hemisphere, the new ceiling of 120,000 on
annual immigration from the western hemisphere, which went into effect in
1968, put great pressure on Mexico, one of the largest sending countries in the
hemisphere. The imposition of an annual quota recast Mexican migrants as
"illegal."[1] Ngai (2004) argues, "Indeed, the persistence of numerical restrictions
in the postwar period ... suggests that in some respects immigration reform
only hardened the distinction between citizen and alien" (229). The tenor of
the 1965 Immigration and Naturalization Act is not much different from the
Contract Labor Law of 1864, which allowed American contractors to recruit
low-wage workers from Europe and Asia. By 1976, the United States tightened
the legislation of 1965 as a response to long-term migration patterns. The
Immigration and Naturalization Act Amendments and the Health Professions
Education Assistance Act of 1976 required migrants and health workers to
show proof of employment before immigrating to the United States. These
restrictions slowed the entry of South Asian technical workers, but it did not
cease the entrance of family members through the family reunification program, which was intended to reunite U.S.-resident European ethnics or whites.
A third wave of immigrants, less affluent and educated, arrived in the 1980s
and 1990s: Gujaratis, Pakistanis, and Bangladeshis (Maira 2002, 10).[2]

How immigrants enter U.S. history impacts the ways in which they view
themselves and their relationship to the "host" country and the how the future
generations see themselves (Kibria 1993; Portes 1995; Waters 1996; Zhou 1997).
Modern immigration policies helped to construct a bimodal distribution of the
South Asian population—the post-1965 group, consisting of highly educated
and financially successful members, and the post-1980 group, largely working
class, including undocumented workers (Dasgupta and Warrier 1997; Prashad
2000; Maira 2002)—and subsequently the myth of the model minority.[3] Part

---

1 In 1964, the U.S. and Mexican government-instituted Bracero program of 1942 ended, a
   program under which more than three million Mexicans—and many Blacks from the
   Caribbean—entered the United States to labor in the agricultural fields (Massey 2002).
2 Some immigrants came through the Immigrant Visa Lottery, which was part of the 1990
   Immigration Act (Leonard 1997). Under the lottery program, 55,000 people are randomly
   selected by computer each year for purposes of achieving diversity from countries with low
   percentages of immigration to the United States. Applicants must meet certain educational
   and financial requirements to be eligible. In addition, employers must certify a migrant's
   eligibility for labor before hiring him or her.
3 The "model minority" trope is tied to the end of the Asiatic exclusion, the post-1965 influx
   of Asian immigrant professionals the arrival of wealthy elites from Hong Kong, South Korea,
   and Singapore (Ngai 2004).

of the myth is sustained by the small group of second-wave immigrants who
have done extremely well (Zhou 1997; Prashad 2000; Ngai 2004; Kwong and
Miščević 2005), but eliding the image of the model minority as a politically and
historically contingent social construction is a misstep. Bashi (1998) argues the
model minority cannot be spoken of as an essentialist category that adheres
to the Asian American category (960). Maira (2002) shares the image of the
model minority is contingent upon a small cohort of the overall immigrant
group. Ignoring anti-immigrant sentiments and the myths about American
success, opportunity, and mobility,[4] Prashad (2000) offers that the model
minority image persists because most desi immigrants tend to disregard racism in civil society[5], and they follow an old tradition that group Indians with
"whites" in a racial family called "Aryan."[6] Additionally, South Asian immigrants
firmly believe in the myth of meritocracy, that education and hard work wash
away structural barriers to success, and American exceptionalism.[7] While most
South Asians envisioned making enough money, educating their children, and
then returning to their homelands for retirement (Prashad 2000), many post-
1965 immigrants, like the Punjabi pioneers, remained to raise their families in
America.[8]

4 The model-minority image exacerbates the threat of competition among older residents
   or citizens, and economic frustration among unemployed laborers fans racial antagonism,
   leading to violent assaults against South Asians. In 1987, youth gangs known as Dot Busters
   (in reference to the bindi some South Asian women wear in the middle of their foreheads)
   attacked and murdered several members of the community in Jersey City (Prashad 2000).
5 Like Bashi (1998) found among West Indian immigrants, South Asians who have a social
   referent of what it was like "back home" and are part of a strong diasporic network have
   resources that mediate the effects of racism and racial stratification.
6 As part of U.S. anti-Blackness, desis feel that they do not "earn" racism like American Blacks
   (and Latinos) (Prashad 2000).
7 In 1995, the Glass Ceiling Commission reported that despite high qualifications, Asians did
   not rise within their firms or institutions (Prashad 2000) and Hyun (2005) exposed both
   personal and organizational barriers to success for Asians in corporate America. While most
   Indians immigrants did not find work commensurate with their qualifications, rumors of
   opportunity, success, and rapid mobility circulate among desis and hopefuls "back home."
8 The first desis came to North America in the late 1700s as workers on Yankee clipper ships
   that traded between New England and India (Prashad 2000). More arrived decades later as
   indentured servants, and in the wake of the indenture migration came a "tide of turbans,"
   or Punjabis, to the west coast. Between the late 1800s and early 1900s, more than six thousand Punjabis entered the United States through Canada, Washington, and then California
   (Prashad 2000). Many Punjabis who ended up in California had served overseas in the British
   Indian army or as police in China and crossed the Pacific for better wages in railroad, lum-
   bering, and agricultural work. On arrival in California, a few sold tamales from carts in San
   Francisco, but the majority began as migrant laborers, moving in groups with a "boss man"
   who knew English and made contracts with employers (Leonard 1992). Indian Americans

Yet, for many post-1965 immigrants, feelings of not belonging to America are rampant (Prashad 2000). The desire for community draws desis to socialize with each other almost exclusively (Prashad 2000). And, unlike the Punjabi pioneers, American citizenship for many South Asian immigrants had a profound ramification on maintaining strong ties to the "homeland" and socially detaching from "American life" (Prashad 2000). Grewal (1993) points out:

> While for some the belief in modernization leads to a rejection of anything associated with what is seen as "tradition," for many South Asian immigrants ... the belief in a tradition, supposedly static and authentic, remains important for the struggles against racism and assimilation. (228)

Desi migrants bifurcate the world into the outside world/the workplace/capital (read as "western"/American) and the inside world/the home/desi culture that must be protected (Prashad 2000).[9] First-generation desis read the Orientalist "east/west" divide as culture/no culture, characterizing the "west" as culturally empty and without morals. While their social contemporaries back home engage with changing sociocultural ethos, e.g., dating and premarital sex, South Asian communities in the United States are concerned with reproducing an ideal South Asian family, a code extols the virtue of a patriarchal and paternalistic system, i.e., protecting daughters against "western" values. In some ways, cultural time freezes for first-generation South Asians immigrants or "Fresh Off the Boat" ("FOBS") and the desi woman emerges within this logic as the bearer of tradition (Ganguly 2001; Maira 2002). Puar (1994a) insightfully frames the South Asian American diasporic expression of cultural binary (South Asian versus American) as "strategic assimilation"—manipulate and maximize the (potential) power of powerlessness subversively (48)—to preserve an idealized South Asian culture constructed within hegemonic U.S. nationalist boundaries. Maira (2002) writes, "Immigrant youth culture raises questions about the relationships of immigrant communities to the

---

became the newest members to be targeted by the San Francisco–based group Asiatic Exclusion League and by 1909 successfully pressured U.S. immigration officials to deny admission to Indian immigrants (Maira 2002). Still, Punjabi men continued to arrive in the Imperial Valley in California between 1900 and 1917 for permanent settlement (Leonard 1997).

9 The world/home divide is grounded in an "insider/outsider" distinction. Some South Asian immigrants may distinguish between "insiders," family members and close friends, and "outsiders," all others. Dasgupta and Warrier (1997) share personal matters are often concealed from outsiders. When a woman, for example, discloses private information such as physical abuse to an outsider, she may bring shame to herself and her family. A transgressor may be considered a traitor and may be sanctioned by being excommunicated.

nation-state in which they live and the one they ostensibly left behind" (21).[10] I finds the question is not about assimilation versus ethnic enclaves; no model of identity is adequate in helping us to understand the complexities of the lives of South Asian Americans in general and in specific, the lives of the women who participated in this study.

2   ABCDs and (Constructed) Manifest Contradictions

What are desis, and what are their values in the context of America? The perceived "east/west" bifurcation of family/tradition/South Asia from work/no culture/American has a profound effect on second-generation psyche (Maira 2002). The faulty Orientalist divide between South Asia and America allows for little sense of complex cultural production, making dissent impossible if youth want to retain their desiness. Mani (1993) warrants:

> Critical questioning becomes aligned with negation of Indianness. As a strategy for managing dissent, it is especially chilling, since challenging parental authority and aspirations leads to a troubling sense of inauthenticity. Women, made responsible ... for upholding tradition, are particularly vulnerable .... (35)

And Prashad (2000) argues, "The failure to offer a better account of cultural capacity of desis in the United States leads [the second-generation] either to [a] form of a cultural individualism or else to a turn to a fetishized U.S. or desi culture" (125). Desi culture, then, is treated as an ahistorical trait and as a fixed, static, and boundaried state of identity. The essentialist world view of the coherent South Asian family tradition apart from the travails of modernity allows desi American families (and U.S. policy makers) to disregard modern dilemmas of family struggle and adolescence, e.g., drugs and gang-related violence (Prashad 2000). How then do members of the second-generation decide or make choices about identities when they do not have stories filled with different versions of the past?

Maira (2002) points to "economic resources, class aspirations, and financial anxieties that second-generation youth inherit from their parents significantly influence their reworking of racial, ethnic, and gender ideologies as they move

---

10   Appadurai (1990) foregrounds the centrality of memory to the construction of diasporic identities.

through adolescence" (10). Maira conveys the second-generation's attempt to work out their aspirations for social mobility are intertwined with the bifurcated economic trajectory of South Asian immigrants. Prashad (2000) discovers many young desis do not find the model minority category useful in their lives: children of techno-professionals are expected to identify with "white," bourgeois values, while the working class are expected to identify with "Black culture." The research signals young desis in North America have fashioned their cultural politics around several icons of the Black Diaspora and many second-generation (middle-class) desis use hip-hop as a medium of living and expression (Prashad 2000; Maira 2002). Punjabi bhangra, jungle, and reggae are heavily infused in the music of South Asian American remix artists such as DJ Rekha, filling the airwaves and clubs of New York City on a regular basis.[11] Maira (2002), in her study of second-generation Indian Americans in Manhattan in the mid-1990s, worked to discover the deeper meaning that this distinct "remix" Indian youth subculture—characterized by music and dance combining Hindi film music and bhangra with American rap, techno, jungle, and reggae—had for young South Asian Americans and the role it played in helping them to define their ethnic identity and gender relationships. Maira uncovered the youth are eager participants in conservative hegemonic politics of cultural authenticity or the "politics of ethnic authenticity" (11). Most of her interview participants self-identified as "Indian" rather than "American" or a hyphenated "Indian-American" (3). A "good Indian-American" is a person who watches and enjoys Hindi films, demonstrates some fluency in an Indian language, socializes exclusively with other Indian Americans, and embraces a Hindu identity (11). Underlying these second-generation cultural practices is a collective nostalgia for India as a site of "tradition" and authentic identity (12). The "Indian party scene" is salient in Indian American youth culture in New York City and a significant context in which social networks are created, along with the production and refashioning of ethnic, racial, and gender ideologies (12). This space is ethnically exclusive, reflecting college youth who identify as "truly" Indian or South Asian and participate in the "desi scene." The subculture also produces the meaning of "cool" as a New York youth that is worked into the nostalgia for India. In other words, youth subcultures are

---

11   While the musical fusion allows for a certain amount of social fusion, both Prashad and
      Maira warn the new cultural products do not necessarily create a "hybrid" youth. The
      only Black people on the South Asian American music scene are security guards (Maira
      2002, 12). In this regard, Maira shows how the adoption of Black styles by desi youth is less
      part of a rebellion against power structures and more about taking a generational stance
      against desi immigrant parents.

embedded in the dialectic between presumably divergent pathways of assimilation and ethnic authenticity (16). Indian American youngsters are trapped
in a dialectic between the "coolness" of a remix subculture and the need to
be authentically ethnic.[12] Both the "politics of cool" and the "politics of nostalgia" are deeply gendered (46). Women combine the sexually provocative
femininity that Indian American men find attractive at the remix parties with
the chaste, submissive womanhood expected of them as candidates for marriage. Similarly, men manage a "hoody," tough, macho mystique at the parties
with the requisite professionally bound image. The role of remix music is a
critical site in which ethnicities are reinvented and gender roles and class aspirations are enacted. What the stories begin to hint at is ethnic identity need
not be a totalizing identity and can be critically and selectively reconstructed
(4). Prashad and Maira intelligently explore the place of collective struggle
and multiracial cultural alliances in the transformation of self and community to make larger comments on how Americans define themselves, aptly
denoting the inadequacy of current categories and theoretical perspectives.
Both vehemently argue the label "American-Born Confused Desi" or "ABCD" is
a pathologizing term, and they are critical sociological theories of segmented
assimilation that portray urban youth of color as part of a maladaptive culture.
Prashad and Maira offer interventions countering the focus on ethnic authenticity and assimilation narratives by uncovering how the second-generation
display multiple, situational identities that are fluid, complex, and hybrid.
Despite the agentic reinvention, Prashad and Maira are troubled by the ultra-
femininities and -masculinities that are produced by the second-generation.
Maira, especially, show ethnic authenticity are sexualized and gendered. My
research illustrates cultural purity are embodied in a virtuous, heteronormative sexuality that is projected onto women, and queer ethnic identities are
seen as promiscuous and dangerously inauthentic.

Purkayastha's (2005) study on second-generation South Asian American
men and women is yet another important contribution to the discussion about

---

12   Maira (2002) provides two central explanations for the coexistence of a hybrid cul-
      ture with a valorization of authenticity. First, ethnic segregation on college campuses
      demands the second-generation to enact authentic performances of "being Indian"
      versus participating in the coming-of-age rituals of normative American youth culture.
      Second, and more importantly, desi parents' fossilized version of Indian culture and stress
      on its incommensurability with American inform the youths' own experiences of racial
      and cultural stigmatization. The second-generation actively engage in compartmentaliz-
      ing between their "Indian" and "American" (25) lives while growing up. The stories Maira
      shares with us speak to the making and role of insider/outsider boundaries in Indian
      American youth subcultures (14).

ethnicity and racialization in contemporary America.[13] She emphasizes racial and ethnic identifications, even when there is no room to be without a racial identification in the United States, are contextual and negotiable and part of a labeling process. Purkayastha vividly describes how ethnic identification is negotiated by her participants through the invention of "traditions" and participation in voluntary societies. Like Ganguly (2001), Purkayastha astutely uncovers "states of exception" within a relatively comfortable and protected lifestyle offered to her participants. While Purkayastha's findings are a groundbreaking contribution to the literature on South Asian Americans, she appropriately extends the multiculturalism debates, I am apprehensive with her "pan-ethnic" identity conclusion. My informants tell me there is a strong distinction between "Asian" and "South Asian" in the United States.[14] Song (1998) examines how race and ethnic boundaries intervene in the process of building pan-ethnic identities. Analyzing Pakhar Singh's killing of two white agents, Song points to institutional reasons that no Japanese-Indian coalitions—a truly pan-ethnic formation—developed, even though the two groups were subject to the same discriminatory laws.[15] Nonetheless, Purkayastha teaches me racial and ethnic identity is a fluid, malleable, and layered phenomenon that depends on context.

The literature provides a fertile framework in which I can astutely articulate how much more difficult life becomes for second-generation South Asian American women. Community, media, and psychological discourses continue to pathologize second-generation South Asian Americans as ABCDs. The ABCD trope represents an unclear or illegitimate category. They are in-betweens, straddling the Occident and the Orient, and marked by confusion, as the initialism suggests. The fundamentals of multiculturalism are important here: The one-dimensional model indicates that responses are formulated specifically so that one must situate oneself with respect to the presumed unity of the social worlds (extreme assimilation/the melting pot) versus the alternative

---

13   Purkayastha (2005) includes the first cohort of the 1.5 generation (ages six to thirteen) in the category "second-generation."

14   Kibria's (2002a, 2002b) research on second-generation Chinese and Korean Americans uncover similarities between South Asian Americans and Chinese and Korean Americans. Kibria's insights include hyphenated identities as points of assimilation and homogenized definitions of Asian and South Asian values (e.g., family, education, and work) that dovetail with middle-class white America's idealized notions of itself.

15   Min and Hong (2002) and Min and Kim (2002) extensively map the contours of ethnic self-identities among second-generation Asian Americans and the evidence shows primordial ties and socialization and cultural, social, and political integration are instrumental in structuring ethnic identity preferences among Asian Americans.

conception of society as a collection of discrete and divided ethnic and racial communities (extreme multiculturalism) (Hartmann and Gerteis 2005, 220). The identity label ABCD can make sense only within a rigid socially constructed cognitive framework, one that demarcates "American"—the Us—from the "South Asian"—the Other—as mutually exclusive. Why else would the term "Confused" be placed between "American-Born" and "Desi?" ABCDs are perceived as occupying an ambiguous space. Puar (1994a) points out dominant white gazes facilitate the discourse of relational differences between American and South Asian along cultural and generational lines. Gupta (1998) writes colonial discourses "bequeathed a set of dichotomies that were unusually 'productive' in a Foucauldian sense because they enabled the construction of a sociology built on them" (9). The deployment of Orientalist categories in contemporary American society is subjectively experienced by second-generation South Asian Americans and it implies an unbridgeable cultural and generational divide based on U.S. racial and ethnic structures. The deployment of Orientalist categories overlooks that generational conflict exists in all cultures and across cultures (Puar 1994a). The Eurocentric polarized mutually exclusive identity model supports erroneous monolithic experiences for second-generation South Asian Americans. Furthermore, the treacherous American/South Asian dichotomy encompasses restrictive normative gender ideologies. Maira finds conflicted beliefs about women's sexuality and appropriate and acceptable expressions of the feminine persona—submissive and obedient versus the seductress—and gender conflict resolution reinforces gender ideologies. The pressure to be "American" or "South Asian," including the coerciveness of being ultra-feminine and -masculine, is a general strand that can be drawn from earlier studies. Clearly, the tools and choices available within Orientalist practices are not neutral and unidimensional technologies.

In this study, I redirect the debate about the role of race and ethnicity within the South Asian American community. The experiences of my research participants are inadequately reflected by the rigid opposition between South Asia and America. Hartmann and Gerteis (2005) are astute in challenging the one-dimensional multiculturalism model with unity or assimilation on one end of the continuum and diversity or fragmentation on the other:

> There are, in our view, a number of connected problems with this negative, one-dimensional conception of multiculturalism. One issue is the static and narrow conception of social order that it implies. At the same time, it becomes difficult (if not impossible) to appreciate the values, benefit, and even functional necessity of difference in modern societies. (220)

The data reveal that my informants compartmentalize their identities only to reflect more complex processes of sustaining both an imagined South Asianness and U.S. assimilation. The women employ front-staging and back-staging (Collins 2004), highlighting certain aspects of their identities while de-emphasizing others spatially and temporally or contextually to intentionally curate a unified self-identity. The self-conscious exploration and construction of identity is what Gans (1979) would call "ethnic revival" (Maira 2002, 3–4). The women deliberately underscore multiple alliances/hybrid identities (Anzaldúa 2001). Plainly put, the women who emerged out of this study are neither atomized individuals nor are they "structural dopes." Like the Bangladeshi women workers in Kabeer's (2000, 3271) study, the twenty-five women I interviewed are individuals whose preferences and priorities reflect their own unique subjectivities and histories (self-identity) while also bearing the imprint of their own complex social relationships (social identity), which determine their place in society (Byrne 2003, 4). I find that my respondents express their identities in binary terms and perceive their cultural location within a dichotomy of South Asianness and Americanness, but I also uncover the second-generation women are involved in complex processes that uphold an imagined "true" South Asian culture within the boundaries of U.S. hegemonic nationalism and a desire for "Americanization." Jain (2005) uses the term "cosmopolitan post-humans" to describe the imagination of oneself beyond a fixed identity (4). This study calls for a fuller conception of multiculturalism that breaks down the weak and inchoate opposition between unity and difference and between solidarity and diversity (Hartmann and Gerteis 2005). The question then is not about assimilation versus ethnic enclaves: I find that no model of identity is adequate!

CHAPTER 3

From Research to Process
Social Research, Feminist Scholarship, and Women's Subjectivities

In this chapter, I explore the "process" of my research. I use the term "process" because from the point of imagining the study to the point of completion, how I envisioned the design of the study and myself in the role of the "researcher" changed dramatically (Puar 1993). I contemplate the following question: *What do the women's stories suggest methodologically?* As the "data collection" progressed, I became acutely aware that the soulful testimonies of the twenty-five women I worked with over a course of one year are coming from their hearts and bodies. And as I wrote about and circulated the testimonies, I began to grapple with some of the problems of not only my role as a storyteller but also how narratives are told by academics, along with the media, popular fiction writers, and the cinema. For instance, the use of the category ABCD automatically dictates a staccato (auto)biographical trajectory. In the ABCD framework, diasporic spaces are defined by difference: South Asia is perpetually seen as a site of the problem, the second-generation are constructed as confused and in transition (into assimilation), as in Bharati Mukherjee's *Jasmine* (1989), and the United States and freedom are nearly synonymous. I learn that the women's testimonies are living proof of history (Brooks 2007) and my respondents, through their lived experiences, unveil the falsity of unnatural dichotomies. My central concern as a researcher is with knowledge production. Mirchandani (2004) notes,

> The difficulties of attaining knowledge because of the assumption-bound nature of science, the difficulties of communication knowledge because of representational quality of the language we use to describe it, and the difficulties generally in the search for universal, well-founded truths. (109)

I am apprehensive about how I may have affected the subjectivities and identities of the twenty-five women I interviewed (Brooks 2007). How are the women's subjectivities summoned and then dissipated? How can I tell their stories without causing violence to their words within the context of theory? By asking such questions, I am implicating myself—as a Woman of Color, as a second-generation, as a Bangladeshi/"South Asian", as an American, as a confidant, as a friend, as a fictive kin or sister, and finally as a social scientific feminist researcher—with the women's telling of history. That is, I locate myself in the context of multiple and contradictory loyalties (Naber 2006, 89).

1   Researching Dislocated Women

Feminist scholars have raised profound questions about the standard practices of social research. Arguing that established methods too often ignore and obfuscate social oppression, feminist researchers search for approaches that will more adequately represent marginalized groups and the social processes that organize their lives (DeVault 1999). In thinking about social research, feminist scholarship, and the subjectivities of Women of Color, I ask, how do I begin to approach my research process? In a similar fashion to Brekhus (2003), the approach I adopt in my fieldwork lies in "grounded theory" (Glaser and Strauss 1967). The grounded theory perspective requires data-driven analysis rather than a priori hypothesis. Moreover, research questions do not shape the data. Rather, research questions are formal neutral questions without a theoretical agenda (Glaser 1992). That is, I use a "bottom-up" approach (à la Simmel), asking how various forms of identity are experienced and understood by individuals and focusing on the words and labels my respondents use to describe their identities. Jones (2001) writes: "Identity, after all, provides an answer to the perennial human question, "Who am I?" Because ... identities are social constructions, empirically examining the role individuals play in constructing ... identity makes sense" (6). When I began interviewing my willing informants in 2004, I employed types of open-ended questions that would allow my interviewees to dictate the substantive topics of the interview (Jones 2001; Brekhus 2003). Classical ethnography assumes for researchers the power to define and represent without challenge from the research subjects (DeVault 1999, 188). An advantage of an open-ended approach is that issues emerge directly from respondents themselves. In this research design, I listen to women speak to learn about them, and I engage with them to learn about myself. This process is called "collaborative interviewing" or "social relationships" (Byrne 2000a), "reflexive talks" (Giddens 1991), and "emancipatory research" (Spivak 1988; bell hooks 1990). In this way, I uncover how women are silenced and can speak up, and I recover unrecognized or suppressed aspects of women's experience (DeVault 1999).

Additionally, I utilize an "analytical fieldwork" perspective (Zerubavel 1980). This requires me to theoretically think beyond factual peculiarities of my research or the narratives generated from the women I interviewed, engaging in abstract generic patterns. It became clear to me that a central issue among my informants, as adults, was how much they disassociated from the public image of the disconcerted ABCD. A concern of my subjects was the cultural representation of not only second-generation South Asian Americans but also of second-generation South Asian American women as the composite Third World Woman who is oppressed and forced into arranged marriage. How the women in this study organized their identity across time and space also emerged as a significant issue. From here, I was able to determine "identity grammar," and "shifts" in identity grammar were important to my twenty-five informants (Brekhus 2003). This class of phenomena clearly belongs to an issue of identity. Though, in staying with the meaning of a feminist sociological research model (DeVault 1999), I avoid constructing typologies about the interviewees' identity constructions and/or presenting the sum of results in a tabular format. Rather, like Jones' (2001) study on English immigrants in America, the contradictory evidence shows that my respondents' identity grammars were often highly ambivalent and draw on overlapping and different discourses to conceptualize their relationships to South Asianness and Americanness. The same person's words often emerged on both sides of an issue, and therefore it was difficult to create typologies and/or showcase the results by providing an inductive analysis in tables that generated empirical categories—grouping similar instances of social phenomena—and explanatory concepts—the components of the analytical frame (Ragin 1994). Hence, I report my analyses in a thematic way rather than attempting to account for differences among them (Jones 2001). Simply put, the lives of my respondents are more complex than what Orientalism can explain.

I have detailed data about how my subjects are adjusting to a racialized and sexualized global society, and the data provide a wonderful opportunity to experience the complexity of their lives. Here, I consciously choose to use a feminist model, which is a collaborative and non-oppressive research design, building on the researcher–researched relationship. In this research, I use an intersectional approach and anti-categorical complexity (McCall 2001)—a cutting edge method used by feminists and other social scientists to manage complexities produced by nonlinear, intersectional research instruments—as a methodological tool to examine the lives and perceptions of second-generation Bengali American women. Feminists of Color have come to realize that there is one thing that all women have in common: multiple oppression. Some women are oppressed because they live their lives within binary categories and others are oppressed because they do not fit into dichotomous categories. But all women exist on multiple identity axes. Mohanty (1988,

2003), Anzaldúa (2001), and Sandoval (1991) agree to challenge the rigidity of identity variables and focus their attention on the politics of difference. An intersectional analysis allows one to recognize that women, regardless of geo-political location, experience discrimination because they stand on multiple identity axes simultaneously or "matrix of domination" (Collins 2000). An anti-categorical approach has the added benefit of managing complexities of multiple axes that are contradictory. It emphasizes a range of diverse experiences from multiple identities that do not fit into rigid categories. The assumption is that identities do not fit into neat little categories unless forced to do so by imposition of normative orders such as gender and race (McCall 2001). I wish to stress that multiple dimensions of identity cannot be understood as autonomous and mutually exclusive components, but rather they should be understood within a dialectical framework, each identity variable feeding off each other and feeding into each other (Anzaldúa 2001). This research contests an additive analysis of identity and oppression and embraces a multiplicative one.

The ethnographic research helps to deconstruct artificial normative social categories and power relations. The intentional and deliberate research process allows me to bring the twenty-five women I interviewed from the "margins" to the "center" of academic discourse by, first, reflecting theories of power and domination; second, undoing the construction of women as silent and inferior; third, theorizing from the position of the Other; and fourth, embodying and enacting agency and subjectivity by collaborating with women like me and writing about our common experiences. Here, unlike many feminist scholars who outline agency as social or group solidarity and resistance, I define agency as (un)conscious techniques women use to define and create their own lives (Freeman 2000). Finally, as part of the collaborative research model, I invite respondents to read and evaluate the completed product (Byrne 2000b). A collaborative research model does not mean that I give research participants control over the research and the research product (Byrne 2000b), which is an ethnographic text. I am the sole author and I take responsibility for the interpretation. In this way, I engage in small-scale interviews within a feminist research model in the tradition of sociology. While the methods I employ—small-scale interviews with a sample size of twenty-five—do not get me to understand American society and make broader claims about South Asian American collective identities, it does point me in the direction to question modernity and Orientalism and assess how identity is found in a "liquid modern" era (Bauman 2004).

2   Exploring the Unexplored

In this research, I conducted one-on-one in-depth interviews with twenty-five
second-generation Bengali American women across the nation to capture their
life experiences. Each six- to eight-hour interview spanned over a single day,
including meal breaks. The women and I spent a considerable amount of time
together outside of the actual interview in which further exchange took place,
which included, at times, my participation in family events and other social
gatherings. The interviews were tape-recorded and transcribed primarily in
American English, with Bengali words and phrases sprinkled within the conversations. I did not use Bengali words or phrases to describe situations unless
a woman used Bengali first or she gave me a cue that she was comfortable
communicating in Bengali. The semi-structured interviews covered multiple
areas of concern from coupling to work to families to food to clothing, among
other things. Although the guide was used loosely, throughout the interviews,
I attempted to empirically unpack my respondents' perceptions about their
daily social practices in the United States and to discover the ways they view
themselves in comparison to broader American society. Implicit in my interview questions are the notions of "self identity" and "social identity" (Stryker
1980; Tajfel 1981).[1] In the end, the questions served as a vehicle in which I give
voice to my respondents, provide them with a "safe space" to express themselves, and uncover how they see themselves within contradictory forces of
race, ethnicity, class, gender, sexuality, and nationality and citizenship in the
United States.

3   Bengalis in the Limelight

The interview participants are women who were born between 1965 and 1985,
lived primarily in the United States from at least the ages of four to twenty-one,

---

1   Self-identity theory and social-identity theory link the individual to the social world through
a series of self-composed social identities. The former is often understood to focus on roles
and the latter on social groups. In self-identity theory, identity refers to various meanings
attached to oneself by the self and others, locates the self in a social space through relationships (Gecas and Burke 1995), and is often tied to hierarchically linked structural roles
(McCall and Simmons 1966). In social-identity theory, identity focuses on "commonalities
among people within a group and differences between people in different groups" (Hogg
2001, 131). In sum, identity has two aspects: Self-identity and social identity. Like Mead's (1962/
1967) "I" and "Me," these two aspects of identity are linked by the concept of self (Giddens
1991; Jenkins 1996).

and had Bengali-speaking mothers who were born and lived in South Asia until at least the age of eighteen. I delimited my sample set along these central features to create a homogenous group in which there would be "mutual points of unity" between the women (the researched) and me (the researcher) along multiple variables.

South Asia is mainly composed of India, Pakistan, Bangladesh, Nepal, Sri Lanka, and Bhutan (Dasgupta and Warrier 1997, Ludden 2002). In the study, I interview those who identified themselves as primarily Bengali-speaking (or at least Bengali-understanding) regardless of religious designation or ties to a particular geographical location. I limit the sample by focusing on Bengali-speakers. While there is a hierarchal distinction between *Bengalis* (Bengali speakers from Calcutta—Indians) and *Bangladeshis* and between *Bangals* (Hindu-Bengali speakers who migrated to Calcutta) and *Ghotees* (Hindu-Bengali speakers originally from Calcutta), in this study, I use the term "Bengali" to encompass anyone who is situated in a Bengali-speaking family. This gives me access to a group of people who have analogous cultural and linguistic practices, thus controlling my sample, but it also allows me to diversify my sample by crossing multiple countries and religions. Indeed, I collapse categories in the research, but I do not underplay religious, cultural, and geo-political differences (which continue to ignite riots and hatred in places like Gujarat and New Jersey), nor do I ignore the hierarchal differences between Bengalis and Bangladeshis and Bangals and Ghotees. But a common ancestral tongue and cultural practices can on certain occasions supersede hierarchical differences. Prashad (2000) notes the creation of a pan-ethnic group "South Asian" in the late 1980s as a new racial subject resulted from the bridging of ethnic subgroups (Indians, Pakistanis, Bangladeshis, Nepalese, Sri Lankans, and Bhutanese) from the Subcontinent.[2] Mohanty (1993) writes:

> In North America, identification as South Asian ... takes on its own logic. "South Asian" refers to folks of Indian, Pakistani, Sri Lankan, Bangladeshi, Kashmiri, and Burmese origin. Identifying as South Asian rather than Indian adds numbers and hence power with the U.S. State. Besides, regional differences among those from different South Asian countries are often less relevant than the commonalities based on our experiences and histories of immigration, treatment and location in the U.S. (352)

---

2 Dasgupta and Warrier (1997) state that while the countries that constitute South Asia are all separate nations and the regions are not monolithic, they share 5,000 years of continuity in time and space that allows one to consider them as a social and cultural whole.

The history of South Asians in the United States involves the interethnic mixing of sub-populations.

I restrict the sample through birth from the mid-1960s to mid-1980s to capture both post-1965 and post-1980 migrations. Prashad (2000) finds the South Asian population in America is bimodal, with the post-1965 group—the second wave—consisting of highly educated as well as financially successful members, and the post-1980 group—the third wave—largely working class. I am interested in examining the bimodality, gauging differences in class, educational background, and careers. Despite potential demographic differences, many second-generation South Asian children grow up with the commonality of both Bengali folk and Bollywood song and dance. There were not many desi cultural sources available to immigrant parents between the mid-1960s and mid-1980s other than oral tradition and the movie industry.[3] I do not restrict my sample to American birth. Immigrant children are generally known as "one-and-a-half generation" (Rumbaut and Portes 2001) but the emerging literature on the "new second-generation" discusses contemporary immigrant children who have arrived in the United States before they reach adulthood alongside U.S.-born children (Portes 1996).[4] In this book, I define "second-generation" to refer to those women who are U.S.-born or arrived in the United States by the age of four, with a foreign-born mother.

Finally, I situate my study to central New Jersey, New York City, central Illinois, and northern California. In my search for participants, I opened the study cross-nationally, and I received an overwhelming response from New Jersey, New York, Illinois, and California. The four geographical sites are large metropolitan areas with long-standing organized first-generation immigrant South Asian American groups. Between 1990 and 2000, the South Asian American population in New Jersey and New York increased from 79,400 to

---

3 Only within the last two decades, the arrival of an affordable Super Dish Satellite has brought in an influx of local channels directly sponsored from India, Pakistan, and Bangladesh in real time.

4 The use of term "second-generation" is not consistent. Depending on the social, historical, and immigration processes and nationalities being studied, "second-generation" is sometimes broadened to include foreign-born children arriving at preschool age (zero to four years) because they share linguistic, cultural, and developmental experiences like those born here (Zhou 1997). The one-and-a-half generation is sometimes broken down into two cohorts: Children between six and thirteen and those arriving as adolescents (thirteen to seventeen) who are like first-generation children (Zhou 1997). Even though the literature varies in the ways "second-generation" is defined, scholars have agreed that there are important physical and psychological developmental differences in the socialization processes between children of different cohorts.

169,180 and 140,985 to 251,724, respectively (Census 2000). New York City is the most popular destination for many South Asian immigrants (Maira 2002). Similar population growths took place in Chicago. Like New Jersey (Edison) and New York (Jackson Heights), the dramatic growth of the South Asian community in Chicago since 1965 helped to spawn the large ethnic neighborhood known as "Devon Avenue," one the largest marketplace for South Asian goods and services in North America, teeming with grocery stores and restaurants, video and gift shops, and sari and jewelry stores. Even before the arrival of settlements of South Asians in New Jersey and New York and the greater Chicagoland area, the most sizeable wave of pioneering South Asian migrants are the Punjabi Sikhs who established agricultural communities in the early twentieth century in California (Leonard 1997). Therefore, California not only houses recent immigrants, but it is also home to "older" generations of South Asian Americans.

Within the outlined sample requirements, twelve women resided in New York, five in New Jersey, five in Illinois, and three in California. The women in the study ranged in age from nineteen to thirty-three. Twenty-three of the women were born in the United States; one was born in Bangladesh, arriving here at age two; and another was born in India, arriving here at nine months. Out of the twenty-five women I interviewed, seventeen of the women's parents emigrated from India (mostly Calcutta), seven identified Bangladesh as their heritage, and one woman traced her heritage to India and Nepal. The women's fathers were in the medical profession, the IT field, or held PhDs and worked in academic institutions or the private sector. The women's mothers' careers spanned from being a full-time homemaker to part-time teacher's aide to a small group of women holding professional careers in medicine either as practitioners or administrators. Interviewees who are children of physicians, except for one woman whose parents arrived in the United States post-1980, were raised in upper- and upper-middle-class neighborhoods (wealthy and white suburban communities). Children of the technocratic and academic professionals were raised in middle-class and "somewhat diverse" neighborhoods. Consequently, almost all the women primarily grew up in "white suburbia." Eight of the women were married, ranging from newlyweds to married for five years. Out of the eight, one woman filed for divorce and another woman gave birth to child. Of the remaining seventeen women, five were in committed relationships, three were engaged to be married, and nine were single (not seeing anyone) or in casual relationships. Out of the twenty-five respondents I interviewed, two participants identified as gender-queer, while the others self-identified as heterosexual or primarily heterosexual. Educational completion varied. All completed high school. Some were in undergraduate programs with undecided majors, and others were enrolled in master's, professional, or doctoral degree programs. College graduates' careers included artist/poet, advertising consultant, consumer analyst, acupuncturist, textbook editor, doctor, bank teller, social worker, corporate lawyer, and elementary school teacher. During the research, one woman quit her job scheduling medical services to take care of her husband, who was diagnosed with a chronic condition.

4   Access Granted

As a second-generation Bengali American woman, I began contacting potential women for the study by using both snowball and convenience sampling. In January 2004, I approached friends via e-mail and telephone whom I thought would be able to introduce me to potential respondents from their social networks that I was not a part of or had little connection to. My second source was to e-mail acquaintances whom I had met through professional and cultural networks from across the nation, such as the *National Association Bengali Conference*'s (NABC) Youth Committee in New Jersey; *South Asian Public Health Association* (SAPHA) in the Maryland/Virginia area; and *South Asian Sisters*, a Bay Area e-community. I asked for help in identifying and approaching prospective interview participants. I compiled a list of women's names with e-mail addresses and telephone numbers, and I made direct contact via e-mail with approximately thirty-five women who were not part of my immediate social and professional circles. Such nonrandom sampling techniques allowed me to target a portion of the population that may be underrepresented using random sampling methods.

After my initial e-mail contact with the thirty-five women, I emailed the informed consent form providing information about me, the purpose of the study, a statement assuring the respondent's confidentiality, and the Human Subjects Protocol approval number (Rutgers University). Out of the thirty-five women, twenty-five agreed to partake in the study. The interviews took place in a variety of locations, including my home, coffee shops, hotel rooms/lobbies, the women's homes, and my mother's home. (The day before the interview, I called each woman to introduce myself, confirm our time together, respond to questions/concerns and connect to ease the tension and awkwardness for the next day.) On average, I spent eight hours with each respondent, out of which approximately five to six hours were recorded conversation. The interviews took place between January 2004 and December 2004.

My relationships with the women prior to the interviews were mostly nonexistent, except for two women. However, once I embarked on this journey, a handful of the women and I discovered that our fathers were part of the same cohort at Dhaka Medical School or had come from the same district (*upuzilla*)/village (*bari* or *desh*) in Bangladesh or that our mothers had received voice training from the same vocal teacher/*ustad ji* or that we had both accompanied our parents to the U.S.-based *Bangladesh Medical Association* (BMA) annual conferences in the same years. After speaking for less than an hour, one woman and I realized that she was the friend of one of my college roommate's younger sister and that she used to hang out at my campus apartment! Another woman and I discovered that we had not one but two friends in common. Finally, many of the women and I found commonalities in some aspect of our upbringing, e.g., "weekend friends." Apart from my expectation to share some commonalities in our socialization as "second-generation South Asian American women," I was astounded to discover the multiple layers the women and I shared. The collapsing degrees of separation between us were at times comforting on both ends, and at times not, e.g., a respondent who chose to veil their gender-queer identity from their family and Muslim community and another respondent was dating someone outside of her religious beliefs for more than seven years without her parents' knowledge with no immediate plans to tell them. In such cases, women chose aliases for themselves to be used in the study, and I have tried to protect their identities to the best of my abilities. Once the study was completed, I continued to maintain contact with all twenty-five women via e-mail over the years, giving them updates about my life and work and asking them to share new developments in their lives. Through e-mail conversations and e-albums, I was informed about the birth of a child, two more engagements, a wedding, a break-up, a divorce, and a relocation.

5   Analyze This ... Analyze That

I use a voice-centered relational analytic method for analysis or microanalysis of the interview transcripts. Microanalysis involves careful and minute examination and interpretation, and it comprises two components: Participants' recounting of events and the observers' interpretation of those events (Strauss and Corbin 1998). Mauthner and Doucet (1998) push microanalysis further by outlining four levels of reading (of the transcripts). The first reading involves the overall story being told by the participants and the researcher's own response to the informants' minds, experiences, and identities. The second traces how respondents speak about themselves (the "I" voice). The third reading examines how respondents talk about others in their life, and the fourth reading places the stories being told within larger social structures.

Microanalysis as an analytic tool fit nicely into the dichotomous modes of identity, self-identity and social-identity. The second level of reading, the "I" voice, focuses on self-identity, and the third level of reading, which emphasizes how narrators talk about others in their lives, examines social-identity. The microanalysis model is a sound methodological way of listening. I rely on Puar (1993, 1994a, 1994b), Grewal (1994), Visweswaran (1994), and Clough (1998) to guide my readings of the twenty-five transcripts produced between January 2004 and December 2004.

6   Non-oppressions to Negotiation of Power

My methodological choices pose several ethical and theoretical dilemmas. The myth of a feminist female researcher interviewing other women as authentic research, closer to the "truth" through an elimination of structural inequalities is simply not true (Puar 1993, 23–25). Having undertaken an enormous sociological research in an academic framework, the process of conducting the study proved far more complex than just women talking to me and me talking to women. Visweswaran (1994) urges that at a moment when feminism is being realigned along an axis of difference and in which objective stance has come into question as the root of ethnographic praxis, it is important to realize that the relationship between a feminist researcher and her subject is central to feminist work and should be considered at every stage of a project, from developing research agendas to writing reports. Repeatedly, the supposed non-hierarchical relationship I worked to establish exuded differences that were not solely based on gender.

In speaking to two women not quite twenty, I found it was difficult for them to treat me as a "friend," initially addressing me as "Dr. Badruddoja" or "Professor Badruddoja" and switching to my first name "Roksana" did not ease my status as an "expert." By being placed in an expert position, I was able to question the ways in which women were thinking. Similarly, speaking to both a recent college graduate and a woman who just began a graduate program, I felt seasoned as a scholar; I felt powerful. Alternatively, I was slightly intimidated by a woman in her mid-twenties who was a corporate lawyer working in her office with a spectacular view of New York City. With great unease, I pictured myself in my mid-twenties, working long hours as a domestic violence advocate with no office and a stipend. In another scenario, I waited for an interviewee for forty-five minutes and I was unable to reach her on her cell phone that day. I left her a voice mail and drove home upset. We reconnected on the phone later on in the week and rescheduled for another time to meet.

Once again, I waited for her, and this time I was able to contact her on her cell phone and we met for an interview later in the day. Another woman's husband called her several times on her cell phone during our interview to ask her when she would be home. The woman's husband's phone calls disrupted the flow of our conversation, but I continued our interview session, patiently veiling my annoyance.

Almost all the women I worked with shared stories of growing up with which I could identify. However, marriage and religion came to be areas of marked difference. One woman remarked numerous times that she wanted to marry someone who knew what *Gilligan's Island* was. What she meant was that she would never marry an immigrant or FOB (Fresh Off the Boat). This was a source of alienation and Othering for me since I was married to a Bangladeshi immigrant. In this interview, I downplayed my marriage. In an alternate interview, I discussed my marriage at length because the woman married a Bangladeshi immigrant, and she and I had met our partners under similar circumstances. Some women assumed I knew nothing about Hinduism because I was raised in a Muslim household (indicated by my last name "Badruddoja"). In such situations, I shared my upbringing with the women, which included a deep immersion in Hindu Bengali culture. Every time a woman expressed that she would not date a Muslim and/or that her parents would excommunicate her if she married a Muslim, I felt a a knot in my throat. In contrast, when Muslim-identified women expressed their feelings about bringing Hindu men home, I felt a sense of commonality and perhaps even solidarity.

Clearly, I submerge power by "constant manipulation of my construction" (Puar 1993, 25). I highlight areas of commonality I found with women (e.g., talking about my marriage at length with women who were also married to South Asian immigrant men) and downplay differences (e.g., bringing less attention to my marriage when I sensed disdain). In these ways, the balance of power continuously swayed from one side—to me—to the other—to the women I interviewed. Puar (1993) captures my experiences:

> The interactive interview which characterises much feminist research and ethnography is far more complex than simply having someone to share experiences with. An actual interview session itself alone can involve numerous exchanges of balance of power, subversions, unintended and even intended oppressions. (25)

And Visweswaran (1994) suggests that while ethnographies point to description and detachment, the style and arrangement the author uses reflects their perspective on the history and the purpose of the ethnographic text. The process of writing and presenting is perhaps one of the only spaces within the book in which I have expansive power, excluding the input of the publisher.

Finally, my methodological choices call attention to questions about positivistic notions of value-free, neutral, and scientific. Feminist methods, read as qualitative and "soft" science, remain under much scrutiny. Interactionists cast a powerful light on the importance of choice in explaining human behavior, but they have little to say about power and how it might create inequalities in people's ability to choose. Alternatively, structural theories emphasize individual choice but fail to acknowledge how individuals manipulate within these constraints. Kabeer (2000) remarks:

> Ideology and culture do not merely operate as externally-imposed constraints on people's choices; they are woven into the content of desire itself. Consequently, what people need and want, how they define their identities and their interests, partly reflect their own individual histories and subjectivities, but are also significantly and systematically influenced by the norms and values of the societies to which they belong. (328)

Positivistic research methods, then, serve to control data, irregularities of human experiences, and knowledge; while feminist research strategies, such as personal narratives, seek to disrupt scientism and positivism (Lentin 2000). And by articulating individual experiences of the women I interviewed, I extrapolate to the broader social position manifested in the individual (Freeman 2000). Clough (1998) is especially helpful in the context of highlighting women's voices and intersectionality. Clough challenges the observer's struggle to uncover participants' unified identity by disrupting objective reporting/the naturalized male (38). She chooses ethnography as the focus for feminist deconstruction of "objective" social science. Clough treats ethnography as an activity of construction of masculine authority (dead, abstract, and neutral) narrating feminized subjects (independent of the text). Ethnographic writing can rapidly undo the invisible male authority (5, 27, 133). Following in Clough and Kabeer's footsteps, the analytical approach in this book is to acknowledge the research field as a feminine site within writing and structure without denying agency (women's interactions surely shape how they do identity work). I do not claim to present facts in this book. Rather, I showcase competing realities with women as subjects and I underscore common experiences. I am still a modern subject, collecting data, drawing conclusions, and using conceptual tools, but I am modest about the absolute nature of my findings. This study is a dialogical project of contemporary social theory and single moments or perspectives in a changing world.

CHAPTER 4

Racial and Ethnic Imaginary

Projects of (Re)Negotiation

In this chapter, I focus on the politics of race and ethnicity through the lives of the women. I explore how South Asians in America are racialized and how they respond to U.S. "racial projects" (Omi and Winant 1986), including the ways in which the women in this study are prompted to adopt racial and ethnic labels. I do this by searching the transcripts for thin references to racial categories or discussions about the ways my respondents adapt to racial affronts. I find the women sort themselves by contesting notions of race—"Asian"—and appropriating ethnic discourse—"Bengali." In addition, the women in this study forge the label "South Asian" or "South Asian American" as a salient identity. However, their refusal to identify solely as racial subjects does not mean the women wholly reject the existence of race, nor does it mean they get to absolve themselves from racial categorization. Here, the women use Omi and Winant's (1986) "ethnicity paradigm" (15) to talk about race, while they fail to acknowledge that ethnic labels are part of racialization and racialization is a positioning process that takes place within a racial hierarchy (Bashi 1998, 960). Race is ascribed and not asserted (Cornell and Hartmann 1998) and forging the label "South Asian" is just one example of what Omi and Winant (1986) call a "racial project" (56). Labels like "South Asian" or "South Asian American" characterize a racializing process and are racialized labels. South Asian Americans, like West Indian Americans (Bashi 1998), do not have a choice between ethnicity and race. Rather, individuals have both ethnic and racial identities at the same time. The choice between ethnic and racial labels is a false one.

1 Contesting Race

Like Bashi's (1998) study on young West Indians in America, the women with whom I worked with are puzzled about the meaning of race. Some of the women ask me, "What does race mean?" While my research respondents unanimously express that they know which "race" box to checkmark on employment, admissions, and U.S. Census forms, they voice bewilderment over racial categories like "white," "Hispanic," and "Asian Pacific Islander." The women question, "If we don't really know what race is, what is my racial identity?" "What does my race indicate about me?" And "Should I use race to construct myself?"

Indira confides in me that she asks, "the race question" almost every day: "How is race defined and what is my race really?" Indira explains her struggles,

> When I think of race, I think of the boxes on the forms, and if I have to say what race I am, do I have to say I am "Asian" then? I struggle with it ... Racially, I don't feel like I know what to say because even if you look at the history of the census, Indian people used to be categorized as "Caucasian" at some point ... I don't get it.

Living abroad helped Mazeda to see that U.S. racial categories and hierarchies are unique to America (Davis 1991; Twine 1997). Mazeda's experiences working overseas as a Peace Corps volunteer left her questioning not only the validity of race as a meaningful organizing category:

> When I was in the Peace Corps ... [I] was [in] a small rural village in northern Côte d'Ivoire ... A lot of people had only seen the white French foreigners ... or white Americans ... So when I got there ... this old woman said, "She's red, she's red. What is she?" ... Most people didn't know what to call me because I was darker than the other volunteers, but I wasn't like them ... I have no idea [what I am anymore].

Rekha complicates the common Black/white racial schema to understand herself and others around her within the context of a diversifying demographic landscape. Growing up in a small white Midwestern suburb, Rekha simply saw race as either "Black" or "white." Rekha and her younger sister were "Black," a marginalized category in their isolated Midwestern town. After moving to northern California as a teenager, Rekha found she was neither white nor Black. She adopted "ethnic" language to describe and categorize herself and others in her new social environment:

> The color of your skin is what I foresaw race to be. I didn't [used to] associate it with culture very much ... Race was much Black and white to me. If someone is dark, they're dark ... there is no question in my mind ... After living in [California] for a while, I actually altered that somewhat because I see more types of people here and groups of people that behave in different ways, which I just hadn't really encountered very much [in the Midwest] ... Ethnicity is you have some kind of context around [it]...

there is something more than just the color of your skin that's defining who you are. There is some cultural aspect to you or your group of people that you are familiar with that make you....

Rekha's testimony foretells a central theme in this chapter: The women reject race as a conceptual category and a tool for social stratification. Instead, most women chose to locate themselves within ethnic categories like "Bengali." The women find that a "Bengali" identification provides them with the reflexivity they are searching for in constructing their self-identities.

In this study, the women define ethnicity through language, foodstuff, customs and traditions, and ancestral heritage. Rupa makes clear to me that even though her parents were born and raised in the geographical area that is now Bangladesh, she traces her heritage to multiple migrations between India and Bangladesh. To encompass both India and Bangladesh in her self-definition, Rupa uses "Bengali" to describe her ethnicity. Rupa says, "In my bio, I identify as 'Bengali-American-Islam.'" Rani connects her ethnic identity to song and dance, food, clothing, and Bollywood. She also labels herself as a Bengali: "[If] I'm in a group of Indians and I say, "Oh, I'm Bengali," then they say, "Do you sing and dance?"...Bengalis are known to be poetic and very intellectual, so those labels come along with being Bengali." Padmini, like Hasnat (1998), articulates her ethnicity as Bengali through the relationship between food and identity. For Padmini, being "American" is absolutely about eating fried chicken (whiteness) and being "Amreekan" is about eating chicken tikka (brownness):

> I think this remains a place where white is pretty, where accents are funny, and food that smells strong is gross and weird ... I try to deny it and I'm like, "No, I'm sure they're all liberated. Like even in Kentucky, they're all eating curry ..." But they're not. They like McDonald's ....

Auditi adroitly links her ethnicity to belonging to and participating in a community that is composed mostly of Hindu Bengali immigrants and their American-born and/or raised children:

> When I think of myself as a Bengali American, I am thinking of myself as an insider of a particular community ... It was a more safe or comfortable place where you didn't necessarily have to deal with the issues of being an outsider and having to fit in this little white high school community. In a way, when I would go to Bengali events or when I was with my family and everybody's speaking Bengali, those conflicts that were part of being a child of immigrant's kind of went away.

Auditi sees herself as Bengali American.

The women vividly detail ethnic identities that are connected to the sights, sounds, and smells of "chicken tikka." The women immerse their identities in political, historical, cultural, and ancestral ties, adopting ethnic labels instead of racial ones. The use of ethnicity as a conceptual category is an active and conscious decision on the part of the women. Stories of heritage and culture resonate through the women's voices. Shankar and Srikanth (1998) emphasize the process of ethnic construction and point to the emergent nature of ethnic identity. Ethnicity is fragmentary, contradictory, and an elusive variable, but, nevertheless, it evokes considerable emotional loyalty among individuals and groups. My research participants find that formulated racial boxes prevent them from realizing their links to multiple geographies, peoples, and customs. In this way, the women rupture U.S. nationalism and its partner, a universalizing South Asian category, through ethnic identification. Kibria (1998) and Bashi (1998) push back; they profess ethnic construction is an illusion. Discarding race as a defining category does not mean that "race" no longer matters in the women's lives. The women's words echo Omi and Winant's (1986) ethnicity paradigm, which assumes that "race" is just one of the numerous determinants of ethnicity and highlights how the racialization process submerges ethnicity as it forces people into racial identities. Race is a hierarchical power structure while ethnicity is not (Bashi 1998, 961). The women's attempts to compete for power (and perhaps even changing the existing racial hegemony) is accomplished within the construction of racial categories that come from outside the group, in which "white" is a power position in the racial structure of the United States (Winant 1994; Bashi 1998). Kibria (1998) asserts that ethnic labels characterize a racializing process, and Bashi (1998) argues that racialization is related to a group's incorporation into a hierarchical, stratifying, socioeconomic system. Bashi (1998) writes, "One is not allowed to be without a race in a racialized society" (966). What I uncover through my interviews is that the women's preferences to discuss themselves in ethnic terms do not mean that they have no race.

2   Racing Ethnicity

People do not choose between ethnic and racial labels (Bashi 1998, 962), rather, individuals have both ethnic and racial identities at the same time (966). Kibria (1998) agrees a "pan-ethnic" label like "Asian American" characterizes a racializing process and is a racialized label. The addition of pan-ethnic labels to the hierarchical system of racial categories in the United States moves us from a bi-polar, bimodal hierarchy to one that has more than two levels.[1]

Auditi describes that a "South Asian" identity simply does not make sense while traveling in India: "If I am traveling in India, [the term] "South Asian" wouldn't even come up...." Auditi points to the "western" construction of "South Asian" as a "new ethnicity" used to organize and build communities in America. Mani (2003) writes, "[T]o identify as 'South Asian' gestures ...to ...the racialized location of immigration in the US state" (119). To identify as "South Asian" often involves a post-1965 immigration history in which South Asians are consistently named the "model-minority" (Mani 2003, 118). Ronica's words speak to how the model-minority as a category is socially constructed, and despite its myth, immigrants accept, embrace, and instrumentally use the model-minority characterization of themselves:

> I definitely think that especially in America there is a very strong idea of what an NRI [Nonresident Indian] is supposed to look like.[2] If you are South Asian and you are in your late twenties or early thirties, you should have bought a house, have this much education, preferably in the sciences, and definitely be living out this ideal that is very much a construct of people coming to this country, wanting to have the best, and thinking that they're a failure unless they make lots of money.

Ronica suggests what Winant (1994) calls "racialization" (59) as she describes immigrant adaptation in destination countries. The forging of "South Asian" and its links to the myth of the model-minority is a racial project. Mala accentuates that ethnicity is not a riveting "ethnic choice" as Nagel (1994) and Waters (1996) portray it:

> We talk a lot about what brings us [South Asians] together. Is it simply a link to our parents or our grandparents? To me, it's very strongly attached to how other people see me. If I didn't identify as South Asian, other people would still completely identify me as such or they would identify me

---

1   Visweswaran (1997) argues that even as we move away from a racially bifurcated system, the centuries-long Black and white polarization simply casts the identities of South Asian groups in America as either symbolically whitened or blackened, or places Asian groups in a mediating position between Blacks and whites.

2   "NRI" is an official category of the Indian government to categorize people of Indian heritage who live abroad. The purpose is to provide financial incentives to Indians living abroad to make direct investments in India.

as Indian ... I think a lot of being South Asian means being identified [by others] as such early on ... When someone sees me on the street and identifies me in their head as Indian, that thought comes with a lot of different sort of associations and notions that are extremely different than people who are read as African-American or Black ....

Racialization presupposes the existence of a racial hierarchy into which new categories are inserted. Hence, by definition, a society's racial hierarchy must change along with racialization. While racialization involves the creation of new groupings, it also serves to reify race, forcing people into racial identities (Bashi and McDaniel 1997). Yet, while Ronica is critical about the monolithic and unitary conception of South Asian based along U.S. nationalistic dreams, she engages with the political struggles that come along with the fashioning of identity for South Asians in America: "I feel South Asian is a political identity and I believe in that identity ... I think the issues are so interrelated between Bangladesh, India, Pakistan, Nepal, and the Maldives. I think that it is very unifying to talk about a South Asia and I feel like I have a connection [with] South Asia." Ronica reflects on the importance of superseding a unidimensional identity like "Bengali" or even "Indian" with a multidimensional one like "South Asian." She embraces the name given to her by the dominant culture, ascribing to it positive connotations (Winant 1994, 59; Bashi 1998, 965). Rupa's identity as a "South Asian" also emerges as resistance. She adamantly voices that what counts as "Asian" is sometimes quite exclusionary:[3] "[As a performing artist,] I travel a lot for shows. We are most often booked to perform at ... Pan-Asian conferences or Asian conferences, and it is [often mostly] East Asian or Pacific Islanders. Here [I am] and people are like, 'Oh, we didn't know you were Asian ...'" Ganguly (2001) remarks on the importance of self-representation: The decision to adopt "South Asian" reveals how South Asians recast their identities vis-à-vis the dominant culture, choices that are deeply embedded in hegemonic discourses of race and nation.

Shankar and Srikanth (1998) explore the conflicts and negotiations in the inclusion of South Asian Americans in the construction of "Asian America." They tenaciously account for the tensions and negotiations among diverse class-, gender-, generation-, and nation-based groups that collectively constitute

---

3   Poore (1998) writes, "The term 'Asian' which should include South Asians, continues to privilege East or Southeast Asians, rendering South Asians as the nonexistent among Asians and non-Asians alike. I have actually talked to East Asians who do not consider South Asians to 'be' Asians because they have never recognized 'that part of the world' to be part of Asia. Rather, they see South Asia and Asians to be off by themselves somewhere" (25).

South Asian Americans. Shankar and Srikanth (1998) document the trouble-some formations of canons that seek to create and represent ethnic communities through a central theme: Ethnicity is politically constructed in multiple sites, e.g., academia and not-for-profit. The women's words are evidence of the important power of race and racialization: As two sides of the same coin—an imagined "true" South Asian versus the universalizing tendencies of hegemonic U.S. nationalism and the pressures of assimilation—my respondents demonstrate they are unable to ignore racial projects in America. While "South Asian" is not a racial category, it is indeed a racial project that is part of U.S. racialization. The inclusion of "South Asian" in American racialization is dependent upon the colonial and postcolonial formation of (Hindu) India as a nation-state (Grewal 1993, 228–229; Puar 1994a, 99). Priyanka explains why she conflates South Asian and Indian, lumping various cultures and ethnicities into one homogenous group:

> The reason that I tend to use "Indian" to refer to everyone from that region, even if they're not actually from India, is that growing up, almost every South Asian I knew was of Indian origin. So, the conflict almost never came up ... Up until college, I knew no Pakistanis or Sri Lankans. [So], the term South-Asian didn't occur to me as being a collective term for descendants of the subcontinent until much later in [college], and by then I just automatically used the term "Indian" for everyone ... I've always felt that "Indian" is used more often [than] South Asian [anyway] ... unless people are trying to be very politically correct ...

Rani states, "I assume when they ask me about being South Asian, they are asking me about being Indian." Anjana, who identifies as a Hindu, deploys a selective assimilationist strategy using Orientalist terms. She professes she will date a Christian but not a Muslim:

> Anything different from Hinduism is bad for my parents. But for me, it's not, except if someone's Muslim ... I don't care about being friends with a Muslim person, that doesn't bother me. But for me to date someone, I think that would be huge for my parents ... I guess because there's always been a lot of bad blood between Muslims and Indians [meaning Hindus], but not necessarily—at least I don't think a lot—between Hinduism and Christianity. So, for me, that would be okay if I dated a Christian guy ...

I am painfully reminded of violent interreligious and intercommunal community Hindu-Muslim riots in India (e.g., Gujarat in 2002), and despite

Hindu-Christian riots, Anjana's strategy disassociates South Asian Christians from South Asian Muslims, linking South Asian Christians with modernity. Naber (2006) suggests the desire for middle-class U.S. nationalist notions of identity affirms that to be "modern" and "American" is to be "Orientalist" (107). Then, "South Asian" relies on a homogenous category that is situated in hegemonic U.S. nationalist discourse.

The conflation of "South Asian" and "Hindu Indian" is partially due to the creation of a "South Asian Diaspora." The myth of a homogenous and cohesive collectivity consolidates differences (Puar 1994a). While it is important to form coalitions in the United States based on numbers (Mohanty 1988; Prashad 2000), the structural integrity "South Asian" and "South Asian Diaspora" are established through a "middle-class Hindu subject as its normative referent" (Puar 1994a, 101).[4] The cultural category "South Asian" is, therefore, often conflated with "Hindu Indian" (tied to transnational capitalism). It reifies India as the point of origin and as the site of production of authentic culture (Puar 1994a, 102).[5] Grewal (1993) points to the problems of Hindu Indian nationalism, "Some Indian elites, gaining power through Nationalist struggles in India, make alliances with the white, upper classes as immigrants in the U.S." (232). The formation of South Asians as a group in the United States volleys among nationalist politics of contemporary Hindu India, colonial discourses, and new affiliations demanded by the immigrant context (Grewal 1993, 231). Priyanka, Rani, and Anjana's stories highlight what Grewal (1994) calls the "problems of the postcolonial" (47–51). The language of identity when depleted of its political implications can be counterproductive to community organizing because it strips the intricacies of different struggles.[6]

---

4   British conquest opened the age of modern imperialism, changing the content of old social identities—agrarian based—to positioning new ones along national lines. Literate urban cultural activists—mostly Brahmans—produced national identities (1905–1920) that by the end of the nineteenth century mobilized public support to challenge British supremacy in the name of nationalism (Ludden 2002, 141). The provincial public mobilization of national identity around official identities produced strident opposition as Congress called an end to communal representation, particularly in Bengal and Punjab (Ludden 2002, 218–21). The administrative partitioning of states along linguistic lines in independent India in 1956, coupled with the multiple partitions of the war-torn area, made Hindi-Brahman-Indian ascendancy possible.

5   The perceived interchangeability between "Indian" and "South Asian" is informed by class-based Hindi nationalism.

6   Islam (1993) exclaims, "South Asian is a category fast catching on in academic and literary arenas. However, some of us remained invisible in the new name, devoured by the multicultural zeal. The ideal of multiculturalism assumes that everyone placed in these categories has equal space and voice within and between them. But a new hierarchy has emerged in which certain voices have been privileged and have developed their own hegemonic power

Rupa comments over the uncomplicated, unproblematized, and random racialized marker "South Asian." She is annoyed that differences among sub-groups are erased:

> [Yes,] we are all brown and we all have Caucasian features, but at the same time, people from all those different regions [South Asia] look so very different ... Even within Bengal, Bengalis that are on the further east-ern side look close enough to be Burmese, and then further west they look more like North Indian. It is complex, and the more I think about it, the more complex it becomes.

"South Asian" as an ethnic formation that is part of a racial project hinders any coalitions with disenfranchised groups in the United States. Grewal (1993) writes:

> [The] position of dominance in India, together with the acculturation in the U.S., where stereotypes of African Americans, Chicano/as and other minorities abound, often prevents any coalitions with disenfranchised groups in the U.S., with other Asian-Americans, and with more recent Southeast Asian immigrant groups, and often leads to an uncritical posi-tion on U.S. ideology of "democracy" and "freedom." (228)

Ronica agrees with Rupa by boldly challenging the South Asian=Indian con-figuration: "I think there is a big Indian supremacy thing in South Asia, like India just dominates the conversation." Similarly, Laila distinguishes herself as a Bengali from Bangladesh (a Bangladeshi), which she argues is distinct from Indian (Calcutta) Bengali (a *Bangali*):

> Growing up, I knew which one of my parents' friends married people who were actually from India—from Calcutta ... They spoke ever so slightly differently, they used different words, and they had a different accent ... My dad has a friend who [is] Bangladeshi and married a Bengali woman from Calcutta. Recently he has been on TV locally to talk about culture issues and [he] identified himself as being Indian. My aunts and uncles were so offended that he seemed ashamed to admit that he was Bangladeshi. So, I am aware of the distinctions for sure ... I use[d]

... I wanted to know why Indian Americans wanted to claim the term South Asian when they were speaking only of themselves" (242–43).

to always say I was Bengali and then I realized, "Oh, I guess that's not accurate." I was like, "No, I am Bangladeshi. It's different." I feel like I say Bangladeshi now mostly just to not confuse other people that I am from there [Bangladesh] [and] I am not from India ....

Laila unfolds a power struggle and accentuates a racialized hierarchy between Hindus/ Bengalis/Indians/South Asians and Muslims/Bangladeshis, with the latter occupying the status of the Other.[7] Puar's suspicion toward the label "South Asian," then, is not unfounded. She aptly implies while it holds merit as a mobilizing force, it connotes sameness when in fact there is hierarchical multiplicity. "South Asian" imposes monolithicness when the dynamics of hegemony also operate among minority communities; it implies solidarity where, often, there is division. "South Asian" (which equals Indian) "unregisters borders" (Poore 1998, 24). Indeed, the "South Asian" identity constitutes and reinforces a particular kind of assimilation for the women involved in my field work.

3   The Racial Beast

While "South Asian" remains a meaningful identity to my respondents (Mani 2003, 118), I find the women try to self-imagine who they are beyond the homogenized and linear category "South Asian," precisely because the label is prescribed to them as part of U.S. racialization. Rupa says,

> I do feel like my identity is fractured, and I am constantly trying to make it a whole somehow or figure out what it is. At the same time, I don't feel I can just put borders between them. It is not like my arm is American and my head [South Asian]. It is not as linear as that; it is blurrier.

Rupa demonstrates a considerable effort to consider the application of intersectionality and the range of inclusions and exclusions her racialized identity has to offer. My research participants forge the label "desi" to address some of

---

7   The separation of Pakistan from Bangladesh in 1971 forced many Bangals (Hindus originally from the area now Bangladesh) to migrate to Calcutta, and Calcutta became the production hub of high art and scholarly thought, marking Bangladeshis, primarily Muslims, as secondclass. Post-9/11 conditions created an open forum for Hindu-Bengalis to resurface their feelings toward Muslims and Bangladeshis.

the fissures and to better describe their identity politics as second-generation South Asian Americans. Here, the women and I discuss four labels in the context of South Asian American im/migration history—"second-generation," "ABCD" (American-Born Confused Desi), "FOB" (Fresh Off the Boat), and "desi." While the categories ABCD, FOB, and desi are neither racial nor ethnic labels, they inform the development of the category "South Asian" as a racial-ethnic-national formation among South Asians in America.

3.1   Second-Generation?!?! I Thought I Was First!

Second-generation South Asian Americans are often positioned as ABCDs and in opposition to FOBs within the South Asian diasporic context. I suspected "second-generation" to be a significant identity marker for my research participants and as part of the data collection process, I informed the women that I would be using the term "second-generation" to describe the women in my data analysis. My research participants, however, quickly showed me that my inclusion of the term "second-generation" comes from my position as an academic. They were adamant the term is not used for meaningful identity work in their diasporic communities. Mala voices, "It doesn't actually often come up in my conversations to call someone 'second-generation.'" "Second-generation" is not a salient identity label in the everyday lives of my research participants. And while I provided examples on how "first-generation," "one-and-a-half generation," and "second-generation" are used in the immigration literature, the women remain uncertain about generational terminology and confused about the generation in which they might belong to. Rupa says, "I get confused as to what is first-generation and what is second-generation. I thought that because I am the first-generation born here that I am the first-generation." Rani follows, "The term 'second-generation' is really not accurate because we are really first-generation Americans, right? We are the first-generation to be born in America from our parents." Tina explains to me: "I [think I learned] 'second-generation' from the Bengali community [and organizations]. They use the word 'youth' a lot during the cultural events, like 'The youth are going to do this and the second-generation are going to do this.'" I uncovered some of the women learned the term "second-generation" in college in elective liberal arts classes (e.g., courses offered in South Asian Studies), advocacy and community involvement (e.g., working with South Asian women who are victims of domestic violence), or cultural organizations and conferences (e.g., *North American Bengali Conference* or NABC). The saliency of "second-generation" then lies in its use by im/migration scholars like Portes and Rumbaut (2001) to conceptualize American-born and/or -raised offspring of immigrants.

3.2   ABCD and FOB (American-Born Confused Desi and Fresh Off the Boat)

I rerouted my questions about racialized identity work to address my participants uncertainty and confusion about "second-generation" and the women
offered "ABCD" and "FOB" to describe, in part, their identity to me. Tina says,
"It is just a way of categorizing people … It doesn't really matter what 'C' stands
for; it's more raised here versus immigrant." Mala says, "I think among my
desi friends, we sort of just joke around and say ABCD or FOB, but what we're
actually saying is pointing out a difference in U.S.-born or South Asian-born."
ABCD refers to a South Asian who was born (and/or raised) in the U.S. and
FOB means a South Asian born (and raised) in South Asia who immigrated
to the U.S. as an adult. While Tina and Mala categorize South Asians as ABCD
versus FOB, many of the women in this study complicate the seemingly differing racial-ethnic-national experiences between ABCDs and FOBs. Sera, an
American-born Bangladeshi, depicts herself as more FOB than her immigrant
parents because she loves to listen to Hindi music and watch Hindi movies:

> I'm really FOB in a lot of ways. I listen to a lot of Hindi music, I watch
> Hindi movies, [and] I'm on all these South Asian dance teams … So when
> I talk to them [my parents], it's not like, "Oh, my God, my parents are
> such FOBs." My parents have been Americanized and I guess it's just
> the fact that my parents are so liberal, maybe if they were stricter, I'd be
> like, "Wow."

Using a similar discourse, Noopur, an American-born Indian, finds it difficult
to describe some of her friends who were child immigrants to the United States
as FOBs:

> The term FOB … it is granted as being born in India and being in America
> … and not being able to adapt. So, it is a birth thing, but it is really your
> being [able] to adapt issue. Because if I were to use the term FOB for just
> that, there's probably five people I could list right now, some of my close
> friends that moved to America when they were like eight or nine years
> old. You couldn't tell the difference between them and someone who was
> born here. They truly are FOB in that definition, but I don't think that
> they're having issues trying to identify with American culture by having
> moved here.

Sera and Noopur complicate the ABCD/FOB dichotomy, highlighting the gray
space between the two. I find the muddy nature of diasporic and racialized

identity work enable the women in my research to explore identity-making processes that address mobilization and representation. In effort to cultivate presence and voice, as South Asian women who are born and/or raised in America, the women collectively forge the label "desi."

3.3   I Am Desi

Among my research participants, the identity "desi" emerged in the context of national and cultural ideals that they associate with being a South Asian from America. Rupa expresses: "There is some desi pride that goes down and that feels good. I feel more at home with other people who feel equally adrift and equally marooned. It is like there is no homeland ... We are like this floating island." Noopur addresses the potency of the label "desi" in her life: "To me, [desi] is something that we just throw out there in everyday conversation with my more intimate group of friends or people that I'm comfortable with ... I could never call some of my best non-Indian friends desi. It doesn't work that way [So] yeah, desi is huge." Rupa and Noopur's articulations of "selfhood" are key sites where the oppositional logic of self/Other, us/them, South Asian/ American is reproduced (Naber 2006, 92). Selfhood articulated in terms of choice between South Asian and American position Rupa and Noopur's identities as American. Rupa reflects on being desi and its relationship to being American: "[As a] Bengali, I see the term "desi" [in] Hindi or Urdu, and it is "deshi" in Bengali. So, I see it as American English in the way that we use it now ... I use this word amongst American South Asians." She underscores that desi used in this way is a South Asian American identity construct. Noopur professes desi is an intimate label to describe the experiences that come along with being a South Asian American, an experience distinct from South Asians elsewhere: "'Desi' is a slang way of being proud of who you are in a more comfortable setting [with] people [who] understand it and get it. Desi is [sharing] similar-type backgrounds; they deal with the same frustrations; they've got to go through the same things that you do." Like the identity "Chicana lesbian" (Brady 2002, 100), the forging of such classifications—desi—help to establish a distinct organizational category working as a form of dis-identification and a powerful device for anthologies like *Bolo! Bolo!: A Collection of Writings by Second-Generation South Asians Living in America* (2000). Being "desi" raises associations of struggles and makes my respondents feel like they belong in a collectivity, reflecting revolutionary aspirations and histories of a people. The women are mutually vested in discursive mechanisms that allow them to engage with immigration and assimilation (Naber 2006, 90) and attempt a critique of the state, and they simultaneously mold identity labels that emphasize American nationalism. That is, while my respondents' containment strategies—expressing two racial-ethnic-national categories, South Asian and American, in dichotomous terms—emerge as a destabilizing response to claims of a transparent and uncontested billboard of identity, they also show that South Asianness and Americanness absolutely depend on each other to exist!

CHAPTER 5

Patrolling the Cultural Fences

Community Place-Making

"Culture"—shared patterns of behaviors and interactions, cognitive constructs, and effective understanding that identify members of a group—is integral to my research participants selfhood as South Asian.[1] Unanimously, the women voice a distinct "South Asian culture"/ "desi culture" versus "American culture" or "cultural difference." The women's articulation of selfhood is a key site to produce oppositional logic: self/other, us/them, and South Asian/American. My respondents place "South Asian culture" and "American culture" on a continuum, constructing American culture as "empty" or unmarked. The women in my fieldwork polarize South Asian culture and American by drawing on four variables: Familial ties and obligations, ancestral lineage and ethnicity, work ethic and educational aspirations, and capitalism and materialism. While the women I interviewed express the theme of culture within binaries, locating South Asianness in strict opposition to Americanness, I find they simultaneously engage in assimilatory acts. The women protect the boundaries of U.S. nationalism and white hegemonic discourse, which is predicated on delineating South Asian from American, through Orientalism and Otherness. Without a doubt, binaries are central, yet the occurrences of oppositional positioning in varying permutations are salient. On one hand, "South Asian" is constructed along the insider/outsider model, and on the other hand, race, ethnicity, culture, class, gender, and sexual formations are informed by white homogenization and naturalized racial, gender, sexual, and class ideologies (Brady 2002, 6). Binaries are "always more complex than the strait jacket of identity politics might suggest" (Shohat 1998, 6, as cited by Naber 2006, 108). My research participants' distinction between "South Asian" and "American" often break down, suggesting that the South Asian diasporic community is not altogether a different conception of spatiality.

---

1 "Culture is the shared knowledge and schemes created by a set of people for perceiving, interpreting, expressing, and responding to the social realities around them" (Lederach 1995, 9).

1   Culture:No Culture as to South Asian:American

The women I worked with voice a strong sense of duty to family, commitment
to strengthening the family unit through individual action, and responsibility
to be intimately connected to immediate and extended family members. Nadia
shares,

> I don't think America has a culture. [In my] culture, there is this big
> emphasis on family. Extended family is family; my mom's sister is my sec-
> ond mother. Even if I am far away, I still love my parents dearly and I call
> them every night just so they won't freak out ... You can see that in India
> and you can see it in China, but you usually don't see that in America ...
> American people ... don't even call [each other] on the cell. They usually
> don't have that closeness.

Nadia codifies familial fidelity as "South Asian"/ "east" versus "American"/
"west." Mazeda tells me she must defend her sense of family obligation, like
monthly phone calls to her parents, to her "white, Californian boyfriend."
She says, "He didn't understand the family dynamics I grew up [in]. Just the
difference in our sense of obligation, he didn't have that. He is very close to
his family, [but] he didn't have that same sense, and I had to explain a lot of
things to him, and I just got tired of it." Mazeda, like Nadia, interrogates the
cultural dialogue commonly expressed in "Americanization" (immigration/
assimilation) narratives by pointing to a staple (essentialist) locus in identity theory: The individual versus the collective. Noopur extends the utilitar-
ian argument of a homogenized South Asian familial culture. She exclaims,
"[Is it] okay to be able to go out and spend time with your friends because
that's what you want to do or it's a bad thing because your parents don't want
you to?" Noopur implicitly dispatches "being American" means having little
responsibilities toward your family and doing what your heart desires. She
solidifies the immigrant=family values=collectivity and American=no fam-
ily=individualism logic. Padmini describes a larger life event—her (arranged)
marriage—as an articulation of making life choices due to her allegiance to
desi family obligations as duty and loyalty versus choosing a spouse on her
own to fulfill her personal sexual, romantic, and intimate partnership needs
and desires:

> I am married to a Bengali Hindu, and it is specifically because he is
> Bengali and Hindu ... I suppose if I perceived myself more as part of
> the mainstream, I would have the idea [that] it should just be someone

whom I like, whom I feel comfortable with, and then the parents will come afterwards.

The women convey selfhood in terms of a choice between "being an individual/ being an American" or "being connected to family/being South Asian" (Naber 2006, 92), and they consider familial ideology to be a South Asian and immigrant ethos and, therefore, "un-American." However, my respondents provide a counter-experience to the American=individuality and South Asian=family ethos in parallel. Padmini announces her parents did little to help her when she did not have health insurance: "[W]hen I [returned] to the States from grad school in London, I had two part-time jobs but no health insurance from either of those jobs ... My parents were just oblivious, and they bought a plasma TV [instead of helping me]." During the interview, Padmini began to question her belief that Indian culture means being there for your family: "I don't believe it anymore because of the experiences that I have had with my own parents." But Padmini quickly addresses the discrepancy: "I am not saying that Asians are devoid of values, but maybe once they come to America their values are not much better than your average American ...." Padmini's narrative captures her perceived core American values that reflect her sense of (cultural) self. The women unknowingly draw on Bellah et al.'s (1985) Durkheimian inspired work on expressive individualism and divided individualism to talk about community, tradition, and sense of duty, and my informants' assumption of a monolithic whole is intertwined with the white ethnic immigrant myth (Vargas 1998) and how whiteness is typically understood (Frankenberg 1994).

Coupled with fragile family ties, the women believe "being American" means diluted and weak ties to ancestral lineage(s) and country of origin(s) or "motherland." Rani posits:

> I don't feel that the people who are a quarter this, a quarter that, an eighth this, feel like they have lost out on anything ... [People] ask me about me and then they say, I don't have any kind of heritage. I could not be happy just saying I am American ... I would lose something ... I would feel emptier ...

Padmini comments:

> I do feel proud that I am South Asian ... I remember having a conversation [with a Korean friend in high school and] her saying, "Sometimes I wake up in the morning and I am just so glad I am not white ...." I am not trying to generalize about [whites/Americans], like the trash you see

on talk shows or when they talk like this (using a nasal accent) ... [But] it is a relief that [I] come from a background where [my] civilization has it figured out.

Both Rani and Padmini comment on the invisibility of whiteness, or the capacity of whiteness to contribute to a representation of sameness (a fortress of white race privilege) (Frankenberg 1994). Naming whiteness in this way places it as unmarked and unnamed and the invisibility of whiteness makes race and ethnicity reserved for the Other. Padmini uses her husband's name to demonstrate being American (read as "white") means being "less 'ethnic'":

> The way that we all retain these very ethnic names ... like my husband, his real name is Shaam, but he goes by Sam, and I am like, that is so dumb. Like your name is one syllable and someone would really have to have a serious disorder if they couldn't even pronounce Shaam. But that's just his philosophy having grown up more in a whiter part of New Jersey, where you just really wanted to relinquish any ethnic ties ....

Padmini observes what Waters (1990) calls "symbolic ethnicity" or ethnicity that contributes to individual identity and perhaps to family communion but does not create or sustain strong ethnic group ties (Waters 1990; Nagel 1994). Waters (1990) argues white Americans identify with their ethnic ancestry, but white ethnicity is neither deep nor stable. Collectively, the women I interviewed maintain their desi identity contributes to agentic and richly layered self-representation. Padmini pronounces being raised in an immigrant South Asian family gave her "perspective":

> I just think I see this world from a broader perspective than someone who is monocultural ... I think you can just approach things differently because you are on both sides of the coin at the same time. That is a huge thing to gain. You don't have to talk from somebody else's perspective in a patronizing way. You can really relate to it.

Ronica imagines, "I gain a multiplicity of identities and I get to explore all these different people inside of myself. ... I get to be peripherally a part of many different cultures just based on the fact that I am a mixed heritage kind of person." The women in this study interrogate and criticize Anglo-Saxon culture as superior—the "homogeneity assumption" (Vargas 1998)—and argue being South Asian gives them an "edge" over being a "plain white American."

In addition to voicing their naturalized beliefs that American culture has little or no family values; is individualistic and decisions are based on personal needs and desires; and is far removed from immigrant roots, which means having a choice in ethnic identification, my research participants hold that their families taught them the importance of hard work—an ingrained desi cultural value. In asking the women to think about words, phrases, and images that comes up for them when they think about themselves as children of desi immigrants, the women equated America to "the land of the free" while simultaneously describe multiple barriers of racism. In negotiating racist structures and achieving "the American dream," the women in my fieldwork ignore U.S. immigration policies to unfold their parents' U.S.-migration histories as a model-minority story. Tina proudly articulates the hard work=success ethos within a South Asian American matrix:

When he [dad] was working [in India], he was working at an engineering firm. Doing that work, he would have done well, I am sure, but he wanted to see what else was out there and that is why he came over ... His "making it" story is really just hard work ... He would always be at work and made significant progress in terms of his career and building a savings.

Mazeda reiterates the links among struggle, opportunity, hard work, education, and success for desi Americans:

My father was able to leave Bangladesh because he did well in school ... My mom only finished high school, but she works as many hours and as hard as my father does. So, it is very important for them, for us to do well in school ... School is the most important thing for everyone to succeed in ... [My] parents are always working hard, pushing [us] to work hard ... [They are] always telling [me] where they came from and how hard they have to work and that we need to work hard as well in order to do well.

My respondents attribute a strong work ethic and the desire to pursue education as values ingrained in their South Asian heritage and in opposition to American culture. The women derive comfort and confidence from their robust "South Asian" work ethic and educational attainments. Sujata reminisces about summer school:

In the beginning of every summer, our parents would take us to the teacher store ... We would buy math workbooks, and every day my dad and mom would assign us a certain number of pages ... We had family friends who were part of the "summer school." We spent every summer together, and our days were very structured.

Juhi's mother charted Juhi's summers with academic-based activities: "My mother had lesson plans set out from books set for the next class year—an hour for history, an hour [of this], and we had work charts...." Abu-Lughod (2003) suggests immigrants feel they will be redeemed by education and believe their faith in education is the only path to progress, morality, and acceptance. Zhou (1997) finds ethnic communities channel frustrations with cultural conflict away from rebellion, turning cultural tensions into pressures for achievement.

The basic conservative claim that South Asian family structure and discipline account for their families' success elide that political and economic systems are more powerful than (perceived) culture (Bashi 2001). Tina, Mazeda, Sujata, and Juhi's parents arrived in the United States as professional workers through a particular U.S. immigration regime. The women disregard historical American immigration policies that serve to construct the category "South Asian" in the U.S. Prashad (2000) teaches us a small group of South Asians are disproportionately successful in America not because they are inherently more intelligent or work harder, but because of immigration laws. Bashi astutely points out, "What is often misread as cultural differences among racial subgroups may indeed be evidence of differences in adaptations to racial structures, which in turn may be caused by positioning of socio-economic structures" (2001, 216). The model-minority image is a U.S. policy constructed myth and conceptualizing South Asian racial formations in the U.S. through the lens of cultural difference or "having a different culture" is a grave oversimplification. The women's family successes are not a result of natural selection but of state selection (Prashad 2000).

In further positioning South Asian culture and American culture in opposition, the women equate American culture with capitalism and materialism (read as "white," "Americanized," and upper middle class). Rupa presents her older brother as a case in point to articulate the American culture=materialism equation:

> He chose to be as white as he could be. I love him very much, but he looks like he walked out of a page of an l.l. Bean catalog. He is very materialistic. He is an orthopedic spine surgeon and he has the bmw X5. He has all the right things for the American family dream; he was always striving for that.

Nadia notes, "Americanized to me is like apple pie and baseball. It is growing up with TV, speaking without an accent, going to high school, and wearing Abercrombie. [It's] being around white people and emulating them a little
bit." Rupa and Nadia indicate being American means subscribing to upper
middle-class white aesthetics, which include the white picket fence, brand-
name clothing, and designer cars. Being American means not being poor and
the women implicate South Asians in the process of "Americanization" (via
class). Ronica succinctly describes the links among materialism, capitalism,
and being American:

> I have to [include myself as an American], because I just can't be, "Oh,
> I benefit from [class privilege] when I feel like it and can't benefit from it
> when I don't." I [also] think that part of it is the term American isn't really
> inclusive to poor people in this country. Somehow people being poor in
> this country mean[s] that they are acting less American.

Ronica insightfully recognizes how class privilege begins to break down the
oppositional positioning between South Asian and American, shadowing
South Asians who live on the outskirts of the model minority myth along with
poor Black, Mexican, and white Americans.

The (cultural) worldview that emerges from the twenty-five interviews is
a result of socioeconomic positioning that occurred as part of the migration
process of the women's families. As the women receive cultural meanings, they
associate South Asian cultural identity with community, cohesiveness, control,
ingrained work ethic, being naturally smart, and a desire for education; and
American cultural identity with individualism and autonomy. And yet, the
fantasy of a romantic notion of "cultural authenticity" collapses (Naber 2006,
98). Despite Rupa's model-minority upbringing, having a dad who was Chief
of Medicine and growing up in a home with a large, green-grassed yard, as an
adult, Rupa struggled in college with rape, alcohol and drug abuse, and depression. After seven long years, she finally received an undergraduate degree in
South Asian Languages and Civilizations from an Ivy League. Rupa says, "At the
end of it all, they were just glad I got a degree ... I could have gotten my degree
in basket weaving and they would have been psyched." Ronica dropped out of
college for several years because she was unclear about what she wanted to do
in life:

> I had no idea what I was doing at the age of eighteen. I feel like I was so
> sheltered growing up, and my family was so strict that I really didn't have
> a sense of myself, and I spent so much time rebelling against my family

that I never developed the sense of, "What did I want?" So, I really needed time to be able to figure that out....

Ronica's decision to leave school left her feeling alienated from her South Asian American community: "I think I miss out on being able to define myself based on many different ideals of what a population looks like. Like here in America, the South Asian ideal is over-educated, science-based young person ... [I feel] alienated from the NRI population ..." The women report their parents expected them to achieve an Ivy League education—an undergraduate degree and at least one graduate or professional degree—and the career mantra was "doctor-lawyer-engineer." Rupa says, "When I was fourteen, I told them I wasn't going to be a doctor, and they completely freaked out. All through college [my parents] were wondering what I was going to do because I didn't want to be a doctor, engineer, or a lawyer. ..." And Juhi says, "I work in the media so they [the Bangladeshi community] don't even understand the concept. They're like, 'Are you a doctor, engineer, or lawyer?'" The romantic memories of "home" and "homeland culture" and class-based strategies deployed by most of my participants enable them to strategically assimilate to appropriate norms of whiteness (Naber 2006, 93), and the South Asian/American binary ignores women who do not attend "top" schools and pursue traditional educational (and career) aspirations, or worse yet, do not go to college.

Clearly, culture is a spatial-temporal site bound in racialized class formations. Here, I ask, who is producing culture and who is consuming it? What is at stake within consumption and production processes? What kinds of alliances make cultural consumption and production possible? South Asian Americans, as a category, have a great deal at stake in using culture as a proxy for class and maintaining a class-reductive analysis. By sustaining the model-minority status, South Asian Americans produce "tradition," "culture," and "not forgetting our homeland" and maintain the false "traditional South Asian family" despite living in America belief. The ideal erases the history of Punjabi migration in the 1800s and bestows invisibility to working-class populations. Class formations are dependent upon migration flows, and the making of a lower class is the work of dominant social strata (Lash and Urry 1994, 171–92). Prashad (2000), in the *The Karma of Brown Folk*, declares,

But we are good immigrants. We have advanced degrees ... These cabbies, noted one such professional, are "lowering the tone. They are "spoiling things for us," even "ruining our image" in the United States ... "These uncouth chaps, straight out of Punjab, can't even speak proper English— can't even drive. I don't know how they got here. Must be through Mexico

... I don't know why they let them in ...." The new working-class migration is turning us into Mexicans! (82)

Ronica keenly observes the perceived bimodality of the South Asian American population (Prashad 2000):

> America doesn't want South Asians to come here unless they make over a hundred thousand dollars a year or have some super high-power job ... Do they want chaiwallas (street vendors who sell tea) to come? No ... You see the vendors on Essex or Delancy or by Union Square and there is no way you get treated like a model minority.

Ronica's words underscore while the traditional function of guarded borders is to defend sovereignty, globalization seemingly facilitates mobility and concurrently spawns borders that serve to protect a perceived stable and secure social fabric against suspect populations (Shamir 2005, 199–200). Simply put, by focusing on class, South Asian Americans rearticulate their own experiences not as unwelcome migrants to the United States but as a community with significant relationship to the United States.

2   Third World Women: Culture=Color=Oppression

Lash and Urry (1994) speculate the shift from the traditional market to extended channels of transactions indicates a transformed stratification of the core and periphery, one that differs from the classical Marxian paradigm of bourgeoisie and proletariat (28). South Asian Americans are yet another category of commodification that support the naturalized boundaries of the United States (I am not challenging our acts of resistance). That is, strategic assimilation, oddly, is produced through cultural modalities, which is recast through class. In other words, diasporic culture is recreated through production and consumption, and the modern nation gets (re)created through events of the everyday (Bhabha 1994, 209). I find the class-as-culture narrative centralizes the intersections of culture and modernity within the context of South Asian American femininities, gendering the South Asian/American discourse. I uncover the women in my fieldwork use Orientalist historiography (Said 1979) to frame gender, femininity, and sexuality, aligning themselves with being American women (read as "liberal/modern") versus "village India," meaning traditional (read as "backward") South Asian women.

India (a class-based proxy for South Asia and vice versa) first appeared in the popular imagination of the United States through P.T. Barnum, Christian missionaries, and traveling Indian lecturers or spiritual gurus like Vivekananda. In these domains, as Prashad (2000) explains, "India was presented in the context of a generalized Orient" characterized by "images of opulent and effeminate sultans surrounded by oversexed women, animals, jewelry, and the scent of the unknown" (27). India did not emerge in this discourse as just romantic and beautiful, but it also came across as foreign and barbaric. In the context of gender, femininity, and sexuality, my respondents use Orientalist conceptions to link South Asianness to conservative, strict, backward (and at times barbaric), and static. The women suggest the South Asian American family is based on Dasgupta and Warrier's (1997) "abstract model of culture." Noopur says,

> I feel that a lot of Indian American families will move to America and then act as if they're still in India. And they don't address the fact that their children are growing up in a very, very different environment from what they're used to, and that they try to just kind of recreate a little India in their home.

Juhi underscores her immigrant parents' strategic process of assimilation, a romanticized notion of culture (via immigration and class):

> My mother once said, when you step into this house it's like you're stepping into Bangladesh ... I think that they have the sense that they are going to come here and have opportunities for themselves and pass it on to their kids, but still maintain their culture and the way that they grew up. ...

Noopur and Juhi's testimonies provide a fertile backdrop in which to examine my research participants' feelings of embarrassment as children of South Asian immigrants. Padmini describes her parents' visit to summer camp:

> When I was thirteen, I went to camp and my parents came to visit me ... I guess I was sort of embarrassed ... my parents shout when they talk. They don't talk in a regular voice, and it's not necessarily that they are arguing, but that is just the way they talk ... It did make me feel that these people are slightly uncivilized.

Rupa was equally mortified when her parents spoke to her in Bengali at the mall:

I was ten or twelve years old ... The clerk would stare at them speaking Bengali and then look at me ... I would try to move a few feet away, so it looked like I wasn't with them. [But] I was [also] ashamed of their accents when they were speaking in English ... The accent meant that they were stupid somehow, or imperfect ... [I] always [felt] less American, always the "Other" somehow, and usually foreign.

Ronica experienced shame and humiliation in high school: "We are all at a school assembly and my parents don't know how to do the *Pledge of Allegiance* or sing "My Country, 'Tis of Thee" and I am totally like, 'Oh my God mom.'"

The women in my fieldwork link their parents' immigrant nostalgia and status to an imagined South Asian womanhood that decodes America as open/less traditional/less patriarchal/more equality/more agency. Noopur outlines,

I feel that independence is just what America teaches—it's freedom, and powerful, and in general as a country, you get a sense of independence just walking on the street ... [I]t doesn't matter if a woman's walking down the street by herself. It's not looked upon as, "Oh, she shouldn't be doing that." Even midday, sometimes, you can't even leave the house [in Calcutta] unless you're escorted by your male cousins.

My research participants repeatedly describe experiences of being intentionally isolated as South Asian daughters by their parents from American adolescent and teenage socialization patterns. Rupa expresses,

I couldn't do anything ... Even if I went to the movies with my best friend there was this, "Didn't you see her last Friday night?" We would go to a movie, and my dad would check the time to see exactly when the movie got out; he would come and pick me up and take me home ... I felt like I was in prison.

Juhi chimes in, "America is a liberal country, [while] South Asian culture is conservative and stifling." The women share words like "traditional," "strict," and "conservative" with me. Mohanty's (1988) "monolithic Third World Woman" plays a central role within the gendered South Asian/American racialized cultural divide. Like the white gaze, the women in this study read culture as "culture=color=oppression" (Puar 1994b, 24), relating South Asianness and familial ideologies to the patriarchal oppression of women. As South Asians daughters, my respondents feel they missed out on formative "American" experiences. Auditi declares,

I do think I missed out when I was in high school ... [slumber parties and stuff], even though they seem so silly, are important for developing socialization skills in America ... When I got to college, I was a self-conscious person [because I] really had to struggle socially much more than the average American because I missed out in high school.

Juhi says, "My friends were running around in the sprinklers till they were fifteen, and it was weird to me that they were doing that because I was doing trigonometry in my house in the summertime. So, I feel like I missed out on a normal childhood." And Indira states, "That whole idea of a guy coming to pick you up on a Friday night and you go out to a movie—that quintessential Americana—that's not my reality and wasn't my existence." I sense a desire for "Americanization" that is predicated on "South Asianness" as the monstrous Other. The women's experiences represent a gendered and sexualized discourse of selective (family-based) assimilation strategy. In policing their daughters, a cultural nationalist logic emerges: "good South Asian girl" and "bad American(-ized) girl."

The theme of female sexuality circumscribes the ways my research participants imagine and contest culture (Naber 2006). The women in the study share gendered differences in dating and marriage. Mazeda exclaims that her parents allowed her younger brother to date: "We [my sisters and I] couldn't date, [and my parents] didn't like us hanging out with boys even if they were just friends, things that my other friends did while I was growing up ... My brother has girlfriends, and he is open about it ... And it's ok." Juhi connects the dating restrictions for daughters to (culturally) protecting the female body:

My parents didn't want me to even be in situations where those things [i.e., getting pregnant] could happen, so they just sort of put this huge cage around me ... [But] what was so frustrating was my younger brother was going out. I was like, "He's going out with a girl who is like me so by that logic he is putting that girl in the very situation that you don't want me to be in." But since the onus lies on the girl, my parents were like, "Well he's a guy and he's not going to be taken advantage of."

Anjana talks about how she was thrown into the marriage market before her much older brother: "They're not really pushing for him just yet ... He's in the middle of some job stuff ... They just want him to be very established." Similarly, Rita married before her older brother. Rita says that her parents did not pressure her to secure a high-paying job, like her brother, before marriage.

She points to the differing attributes prized for Bengali women and men in the context of marriage:

> I think with Bengalis it is always education for either side, but for women and men there is probably a difference; for women you could put down a PhD in art and it will be respected, but for a guy a PhD in art would not be that highly respected ... In my parents' mind, it was important to make sure that I was taken care of ... It's important [that a woman knows] cooking ... If you are [a] second-generation [woman, it's important that] you speak fluent Bengali ... I have actually heard my dad say that it is the mother that usually instills the cultural values.

The ideal of reproducing cultural identity is gendered and sexualized and disproportionately placed on daughters. A daughter's rejection of an idealized notion of South Asian womanhood signifies cultural loss, negating her potential as capital (Naber 2006, 88), and we will see later how virginity and heterosexual (endogamous) marriage are salient demands of idealized South Asian American womanhood.

The cultural gendered binaries—"good South Asian girl" and "bad American(-ized) girl"—are a result of the universalizing tendencies of hegemonic U.S. nationalism, the pressures of assimilation, and gendered racialization. Naber (2006) suggests, "A binary cultural logic of 'us' and 'them' ... [is] a discursive reaction to the complex dichotomies of hegemonic U.S. nationalism that at once pressure racialized immigrant[s] to assimilate into a whitened middle-class U.S. national identity while positioning them outside the boundaries of 'Americanness'" (89–90). The women's oral histories deploy a binary cultural nationalist logic and I find the binaries implicate the women in ways that unravel the oppositional positioning between South Asian and American. South Asian American cultural spaces are well-crafted class-based responses to a specific cultural desire—the transformational myth of culture as a language of universality and using culture as a strategy of survival (Bhabha 1994, 178)—shaping the women's movements in various sites of interaction, producing and interpreting space, controlling the relationship between space and social power, and regulating the subject–citizenship discourse (Brady 2002, 83–110). Simply put, "South Asianness" and "Americanness" co-exist, depending on each other both symbiotically and as parasites.

CHAPTER 6

Territories of the Self

Language, Holidays, Religion, Food, and Clothing

Altogether, my research participants present five discursive sites as spaces of cathexis in which they produce and consume or "make" culture every day: language, holidays, religion, food, and clothing. Urmila says, "We speak Bengali in the house. I learned Bengali dances when I was little ... I identify as my culture the food that we eat, the language that we speak. It's all Bengali." Anita exclaims, "My cuisine, my language that I spoke at home, the Indian dress that I would wear, the different functions that I would go to outside of doing stuff with my high school friends." The women suggest that they produce their ethnocultural identity continually through the five discursive sites of cultural production. Here, the women in my fieldwork produce several counter-identifications that rupture U.S. nationalism and define their visibility (e.g., speaking Bengali at the mall). In contrast, the territories of the self are also spaces of cathexis for invisibility; my research participants protect themselves from the white gaze by adopting banal norms of public behavior through normative dress and gait and educational, class, and immigration statuses. In other words, like the Punjabi Mexican American families in California (Leonard 1997), my respondents demonstrate the flexibility of cultural identity, both in its grounding in a specific political economy and its responsiveness to situational factors that allow individuals and groups to make cultural choices. I address the acceptance of, manipulation of, and resistance to hegemonic power through five territories of the self—language, holidays, religion, food, and clothing—by an often invisible and marginalized group: second-generation South Asian (Bengali) American women.

1   Benglish

Language is a site of assimilation for my research participants. The twenty-five women I interviewed state English is the preferred mode of communication. English is used more often than any other language in their daily lives. My informants think in English before verbalizing Bangla/Bengali. Jhumpa says, "I work in English. I speak to my brother in English. I speak to my friends in English. I speak to [my boyfriend] in English. English is pretty dominant in my life. ..." Anita voices, "Regularly, I speak English ... I was exposed to [English] in school at a really young age and [it is] my first language. ..." Yet, my respondents are comfortable speaking Bengali and many are proficient in reading and writing Bengali. Fluency in Bengali expands the women's ability to connect in meaningful ways with their extended family members "back home" and with their parents and their parents' friends or "the elders." In addition, a command of Bengali enables the women to participate in cultural activities like singing *Robindroshongeet* (Bengali-language national and folk songs written by Nobel Laureate Rabindranath Tagore). The Bengali language is a symbol of a distinctive identity and a showcase of solidarity for the women.

Jhumpa shares memories of learning to read and write Bangla as a child so that she could keep in touch with her family in India: "I would write letters to *meshos* and *mashis* (aunts and uncles) in India. It was very clear that it was very important to [my mom] that I knew how to speak, read, and write Bangla." Tonima's dad taught her to read and write Bengali when she was eight so that she could sing Tagore songs: "When I was about eight, my singing teacher was like, I should read them in Bengali, because my parents would write the Bengali lyrics in English for me—like that was a disgrace. They were Tagore songs and they were meant to be read in Bengali." Supriya recollects speaking Bengali in the home was a "big point,"

> Obviously, you know English and you speak English, and then there is a point to try and retain the language, and we always just spoke Bengali in our home. Even if we're at dinner and my brother and I speak to each other in English, we will speak to our parents in Bengali ... As a kid, it [speaking Bengali] was a big point.

Urmila says, "I always take the opportunity to talk [in Bengali] with anybody from like taxi drivers to vendors. ..." Finally, Ronica establishes her fluency in Bengali to make connections over and above reproducing cultural experiences and strengthening family ties. Ronica uses Bangla for community-building and advocacy work in America: "I started doing translation for the Bengali Vendors Association. I can use this privilege and linguistically navigate between these two cultures to give some benefit to somebody else." From the women's words, language retention signals the desire to maintain culture, strengthen family ties, and build community.

Next, the ability to speak Bengali is strategic resistance. My research participants use language retention to create a symbolic space in which to exclude the (white) voyeur. The women in my study often spoke Bangla with their siblings, people they normally speak in English with, in public places like the mall.

Anita recalls speaking to her younger sister in Bengali in public so others could not understand their conversation: "We do [speak Bengali], especially when we are out somewhere, and we don't want anyone else to know what we are talking about." Tonima says, "If I go out shopping with a Bengali friend and you want to say something about clothing or someone else or whatever, we just talk in Bangla." The women also speak to their Bengali American friends in Bangla to be cute, funny, or to share a moment with them that is only theirs as Bengali Americans. Tonima spoke in Bengali with some of her college friends as a joke, but it eventually allowed her to keep up with the language while being away from home: "My friend and I started this [speaking in Bengali] in [college] ... Our accent got bad when we went [off to college] because we didn't speak it. We were like, "Hey, let's speak Bangla to each other." It was just a joke, but we actually started doing it." Noopur uses basic Bengali (and Hindi) words with some of her South Asian friends because they share a familiar understanding about certain words and phrases. She cultivates sociocultural camaraderie that she is unable to produce with her non–South Asian friends: "I could start using phrases in Bengali (and Hindi), and people would get it and we could laugh about it. It was just our own little kind of connection." Noopur's experiences of "code-switching"—selecting or altering linguistic elements to contextualize conversational interaction—is a signaling device. Code-switching reveals that social, interactional, discursive, and other information can be signaled through the alternation of speech varieties in their broadest sense (Gumperz 1982). In other words, code-switching introduces sociocultural information in context.

Assimilation theorists place English in opposition to the "Other" language; one must choose a single language—English—and forgo the Other—Bangla. The women make evident language retention and assimilation are not at odds as they randomly interchange and combine English and Bengali (and sometimes Hindi) words or "Benglish." Such "mixed code" (Agnihotri 1967, 89) is used to communicate with their parents and fictive kin (friends of their parents whom they call "auntie and uncle"). Anita remembers: "On a daily basis, when I am around my family, we mix Hindi, Bengali, and English all of the time. We don't even realize we are doing it. Ever since we were little, my sister and I would always mix the three languages together. We had our own family language." Similarly, Nandita says, "Many times, I can't think of the right word, I'll just throw an English word in there and my parents do that too, so it's not odd in any way ... You might hear half and half. Mala believes the production of "difference" is within the confines of the production of the "not so different." Mala, who is not fluent in Bengali, comments on her own use of mixed code, "At home there are a lot of Bengali words that we just use ... so I intersperse them in my English, but it's so Americanized ... that it might even have an

American accent to it." Alba (1992) finds ethnic identity is significantly related to language (and to foods and festivals). He notes attachment to language does not necessarily mean that people are fluent in their "ethnic languages." The use of a few words or phrases represents "ethnic signaling," a reminder of a shared ethnic background (84). Vogt (1954) assumes code-switching is natural and common. He suggests all languages experience language contact, and the contact is an important element of language change. Alvarez-Cáccamo (1990) argues code choice patterns reflect social structure, specifically class structural positions and changing interethnic relationships; signal group membership such as ethnicity and gender; correlate with group roles of leadership and sub-ordination; constitute a socio-functional style, a culturally specific mode of speaking; manage the speaker's ambiguous or dual group identification; and in general, invoke social identities in discourse.

Collectively, while my research participants identify English as their primary language, the women complicate their ownership of English as their mother tongue by using Bengali as a vehicle to participate in resistance à la exclusion/inclusion. And their oppositional consciousness (Panjabi 1997) is positioned within intersecting coordinates of race, class, gender, and nation, implicating my research participants (and their parents) within a desire for "Americanization." This complex identity is indexed by shifting uses of non-standard Bengali and English. In the end, the women in this study use language to account for and give meaning to everyday life. In similar fashion to Jones (2001), by focusing on language, I attend to the diverse meanings given to identities. I show how the women use language to tease out the variations in their identities as they move from one situation to another (Jones 2001, 109–110). Attending to my respondents' use of language provides a view of identity as dynamic. Even within the boundaries of hegemony, the women I interviewed step over the edge of current assimilation and identity models.

2   Masala Turkey

Thanksgiving and Christmas are popular holidays celebrated among my research participants, and much like language, the ways in which the women celebrate the holidays are a product of flexible and fluid notions of identity, which includes an appreciation of "their" culture and a strategic comprehension of what it means to be American.

As a group, the women voice Thanksgiving and Christmas are salient celebrations because they are U.S. government-sanctioned holidays that include preset time off in the women's professional settings (i.e., job or school). Visiting family during *Eid* or *Durga Puja* requires formally petitioning for additional time off. Supriya vocalizes, "We do celebrate the Hindu celebrations, [but] given that we [are] in this western culture, the western holidays take more precedence ... Those are official holidays, and you get to travel. If you want to go home for Durga Puja, I have to take a day off." In addition to receiving time off from work and/or school, the women unanimously state Thanksgiving and Christmas are their favorite holidays because there is an overwhelming feeling of "joy and warmth" over the entire nation. Supriya says, "I like Thanksgiving a lot. We just have a huge Thanksgiving dinner of 40 people. We just eat and chat. ..." Priyanka says, "My most favorite holiday [i]s Christmas because it is festive for a whole month and that particular week everyone is off, and people are getting together." As Americans, the women express they are emotionally vested in Thanksgiving and Christmas.

Yet, my research participants resist being consumed by the white pole, and they accomplish this by infusing the holidays with Bengali traditions.[1] Supriya's family pairs the Thanksgiving turkey and pumpkin pie with commonplace Bengali foods, traditions, and friends: "[We] make three pumpkin pies ...We have turkey, stuffing, and mashed potatoes, and gravy ... [guests] bring Indian stuff ... [We spend Thanksgiving with] the Bengali weekenders. Our Thanksgiving is not with the non-Bengalis. ..." Rani says, "I know in Calcutta for puja everybody gets new clothes ... We do that for Christmas." Like Supriya, Priyanka celebrates major American holidays with her Bengali community and a hybrid dinner:

> We always go over to one of my mom's friend's homes who hosts a Christmas party every year; it is just tradition. Practically the entire community goes to her house. We all dress up in new clothes. My mom usually wears a sari, and I wear whatever new clothes I got for Christmas, which is usually regular American clothing ... It's not the typical American Christmas dinner with turkey....

Padmini recounts a fond memory of celebrating Christmas with her in-laws:

---

1   The women I interviewed suggest to me that the ways in which Thanksgiving and Christmas are celebrated in America are an expression of "white" culture, often leaving out holiday traditions of non-white Americans like Blacks and Latinos. Unanimously, the women in this study equate America and Americans to white and whiteness. Urmila says, "Regardless of whether rap and hip hop are popular in white clubs right now ... I still ... feel like a typical American person is this white sort of mainstream. ..."

> For Christmas—that's like a big deal somehow with my in-laws [who are devout Hindus]—we go to [my husband's] mashi's house ... Nobody wears a sari or anything. Pretty much, people wear American clothes, but then we eat Indian food. They open a lot of presents ... they spend the whole night talking, and they get hammered. The next morning, they eat breakfast and then go home. It is sweet.

Annual holiday commemorations in such alternative ways—e.g., wearing a sari or having Bengali dishes on the holiday dinner table—create a commemorative narrative about events that are detached from their larger historical context (ahistorical). This dissociation of Thanksgiving and Christmas from their perceived religious and historical relevance provides flexibility to my research participants (and their families) in delineating the narrative boundaries to accentuate a desired moral lesson and leave out those developments that might detract from it (Zerubavel, 1995).

I learn Thanksgiving and Christmas are important holidays in the women's lives and their celebrations are embedded in both seemingly contradictory discourses of America nationalism and South Asian nationalism. Together, my research participants respond to the celebrations of "American" or "western" holidays with insistent and imperious renegotiations of traditional images. The persisting theme in my research participants' lives remain problematizing the "east/west" divide by underscoring multiple and contradictory alliances and articulating a complex process in which the categories "South Asian" and "American" are mutually constitutive and exist both as opposites and in unison. In celebrating the holidays, my respondents engage in a process of "cultural reauthenticity" (Naber 2006, 88).

3   Spiritual Ethnicity

Most women in the study adamantly voice they do not have sufficient knowledge about Hindu scriptures or Islamic text—the two most mentioned religious affiliations in this research—to confidently categorize themselves as "religious" or actively participating Hindus or Muslims. Rather, the women labeled themselves as "spiritual." I have found that while there is a proliferation of popularized versions of spirituality, the spiritual beliefs of the women I interviewed are not entirely the products of the religious tenets the women have been born into, but, rather, are derivatives of "ethnic" practices informed by religious doctrines.

Sujata, raised Hindu, talked about the personal and private nature of religion and she describes her religious affiliation by de-emphasizing strict, devout practices:

> Religion is a very personal thing to me. I don't know a lot about the Hindu religion, and I am not comfortable saying that I am a religious person, but I follow a certain belief ... We didn't have certain [mantras] that we memorized ... You prayed in your own personal way.

Laila retains some central principles of Islam without practicing Islam:

> I believe most of the religion, but I don't really practice. I [do] think about it almost every day because I do feel like it is part of my identity to be Muslim—I don't eat pork, and it affects the reasons that I'm a bit more of a conservative dresser. So, there are things that I do follow that play into my life every day....

Ronica, a Hindu, echoes Laila's sentiments:

> I do consider myself Hindu, and I do meditate and pray, though not very often. I don't consider myself very devout, but it is a part of my life and I am into [it] being a part of my life. It is also something that I feel conflicted about because of the roles of Hindus in India and the way that they treat Muslims and other religious minorities. I like the mythology behind it ... I feel like I have built my life around doing things that are good and right in the world, but I am not willing to have them codified by a doctrine.

Padmini and Rani do not "practice" Hinduism either, and yet, both women are intimately attached to a small mobile home temple and a picture of the Goddess Durga, respectively. Padmini, who does not consider herself to be a devout Hindu, says:

> I don't think that I am religious in that I don't pray every day, and in fact, I don't pray at all that much ... I don't say any mantras. I just sort of have a conversation with God. My husband ... he just does everything. I asked him one day, "The mantra that you are reading, do you know what it means?" [He said,] "I used to know what it meant. I forgot." He considers that he is a very pious and righteous person. It became clear to me [then] that I am not into the rituals....

As I was recording and listening to Padmini's words, I could not help but notice a miniature golden temple, an open box of *agar bathi* or incense sticks, and matches. The temple was visible from where I was sitting in her bedroom during our interview. The smoke and jasmine aroma of the incense lingered from what I assumed were remnants of Padmini's morning prayers or her "conversation with God." Rani says, "Religion does play a part in my life but more a spiritual type ... Whenever I move into a new place, I put out my little Durga picture." She intensely frowns, forcing her eyebrows to come closer together, while she recounts a story of her original picture of Goddess Durga: "It broke. It was a big one too. It was nice. It was a beautiful face, and I came back one day, and it was shattered on the floor. I was like, "Oh my God, is this a bad omen?" It was after I had started dating him." Rani's Durga broke after she started dating her Christian (Malayalam) fiancé, a taboo in her Brahman upbringing.

Almost unambivalently, I find the women are keen on constructing religious categories in a cultural context that welcomes both the traditions themselves while it is also alien to religious scruptures—e.g., praying to Goddess Durga without chanting the appropriate mantra, like Padmini, or marrying a Christian while maintaining a Brahman identity, like Rani. The women work hard to de-align themselves from a religious bracket, choosing instead a language of spirituality (read as "not devout") to explain their religious practices and beliefs. The women show how they choose to remember, "fit," and sustain the continuity of religious doctrine is shaped by the way they think about their life trajectories. Hankiss (1981) suggests that everyone builds their own theory about the history and course of their life by a coherent, explanatory principle and to incorporate it within a historical unit. Hence, the women equate religion with spirituality to explain and insert contradictory behaviors into a coherent life schema.

Next, like the use of the Bengali language, the women use the cathexis of religion as a platform to meet and maintain social, cultural, and community-building needs. Participating in social and cultural aspects of religion, like attending Durga Pujas or Eid celebrations, are consequential. Tina comments on the social aspect: "In terms of upbringing, it was limited to Durga Puja, which happened once a year in our community—ninety percent of how my friends were raised. It was just a social kind of event. Having said that, I think I have always been more spiritual than religious." Rita explains her how parents set up potential suitors for her during Durga Puja: "We will go to Durja Puja, and we'll see Bengali family friends. My mom will ask if they know anyone, so that's kind of how it happens with Bengalis ... There are always certain people in the [community] that are known as matchmakers." Sera describes wearing new clothes, eating food, and getting together with community members: We go house-hopping ... it [is] nice ... I [usually come] home [from college], and my mom [has] clothes made from India, so I just borrow one of those ... She makes typical party dishes like *piash* [rice pudding] ... and its open door, everyone just comes and goes ..." Taken together, my research participants do not necessarily draw on their religious affiliation to produce a devout religious practice. Rather, I find religion is a portal in which to build and keep ties to the Bengali community. Puar (1994b) call this "symbolic ethnicity" (34). That is, fundamental to the women's religious beliefs is familial-type relationships or collectivities. Religion provides the women with social integration and social solidarity.

The women in my fieldwork choose segments of religious doctrine they hold on to or amputate. The women exhibit that religion is a realm in which ontologies of the self are invented and reinvented either simultaneously or at different points in time to serve diverse personal and community agendas (Zerubavel 1995). Gans' (1979) understanding of "symbolic ethnicity" provides insight into the identity processes taking place in the women's experiences: "[Symbolic ethnicity] is characterized by a nostalgic allegiance to the culture of the immigrant generation, or that of the old country; a love for and a pride in a tradition that can be felt without having to be incorporated in everyday behavior (9)." I argue, then, the religious practices described here have been reinvented in the American context and linked to American ideals. Using spiritual discourse, the women engage in selective decapitation of religious rites and rituals while simultaneously solidifying their social ties to the Bengali community. The binary myth between South Asian and American simply breaks down to a decisive cultural force consistently (Zerubavel 1995).

4   Not Village India

The practice of cooking varies widely for my research participants. Some women do all the cooking, some share the cooking equally with their partners, and some do not cook at all. Sujata had a large cheese and fruit platter designed on her coffee table to share with me during the six-hour interview. Tina's husband prepared *iftar* to share with me and Tina, who was pregnant at the time, and he insisted I have a cup of tea and chocolate and hazelnut-filled pirouettes before I left their home on a chilly November evening. Anjana, a doctoral candidate in New York, shared a small apartment hen with a roommate and the roommate's bedroom spilled into the kitchen. Anjana was uncomfortable making herself dinner, let alone preparing and sharing a home-cooked meal with me. Three and a half hours into our interview, we were both in dire need of sugar, caffeine, and carbohydrates; we headed toward the corner *Dunkin Donuts* to attend to our sleep deprivation and dropping sugar levels. Despite displaying a variety of cooking practices and relationship to food, the women in this study demonstrate a consistent trend: cooking, historically, has been an essential part of women's reproductive labor, identity, and power (Counihan 2004, 79), and food preparation is one realm where the production of racial resistance and counternarratives are far less important for my research participants. My research respondents' experiences both speak to the historical role of food production, reproduction, and gender. The women's expressions of discontinuity (Zerubavel 1991, 7) in narratives of food preparation hint to selective assimilationist strategy that reproduces the sexual politics of colonial fantasy—modern:American woman/backward:South Asian/Orientalist woman (Naber 2006, 107).

The women framed cooking within Orientalist terms, racialized and sexualized. Padmini coldly says,

> Bengali food is so labor intensive. It's from hell. It just seems like American people cook in twenty minutes. Life is easier. It seems to me, being Indian imbues a domestic life with a lot more pressure on women. ... I suppose in some weird way my in-laws just hope that one day I am going to pick up that bottle of mustard oil and start cooking. [But] as I got married, I realized that I am not traditional. I am not village India that lives in Bengal. ...

Rita laughs as she talks about a matrimonial advertisement her parents wrote for her (marriages among "educated" South Asians are sometimes arranged through matrimonial advertisements in South Asian American newspapers like *India Abroad*):

> [For] hobbies, my dad [wrote,] "reading, writing, and loves to cook." I do love to cook, but not the way they are putting it down. I was so insulted by that ... I know with my parents the cooking wasn't really a big deal to them, but a lot of Indian or Bengali [parents] that [write ads] for women, it's [cooking] important. That's why my parents probably put it in that profile.

Juhi communicates in an agitated voice, "My mom is trying to get me to [cook] lately. I think in her attempt to make me the perfect wife." The women equate Third World Woman=food=family. Here, my respondents step away from using food as an essential part of their labor, identity, and power as South Asian women. Auditi comments on the historical relationship between women and food and preparation, and how her first date ruptured the boundary between men and food and cooking. She shares a memory with me about her first date with her now-husband: "He cooked me dinner, which for me was a big thing ... It was really a nice dinner. It wasn't anything totally fancy, but it was really nicely laid out, wine and everything...." Auditi not only illustrates her appreciation for the precision required in the formation of a "nice" meal, but she also points to the gendered boundaries infused in food and cooking, "A man cooking dinner! ... That was [a] big thing that set him apart." Auditi's husband continues to do the bulk of the cooking in their family: "I come home and do some chores, like cleaning or whatever, I do a little bit of reading, and I watch the news. I make dinner or, more likely, [he] comes home and makes dinner. He's the cook in the family. I don't really do much of the cooking." Supriya's busy work schedule and her cosmopolitan, single, New York City lifestyle, prevents her from frequenting the kitchen: "I don't really cook that much because when I do go home, it is eight or so. I am hungry then, and I don't have the patience to make something and wait another half hour to eat it ... I honestly can't remember when I turned on my stove because I am okay with salad." Supriya skillfully leaves the "real" cooking to her boyfriend, "[My boyfriend] is a more adventurous cook than I am. He will make fancy pork chops and salmon with a coating that he made." Rani says, "I can't cook. That was always my staple answer, but [my fiancé] cooks. So, when we got together, he was cooking a lot for me. He took a cooking class. He made me Thai chicken, he made me shrimp, [and] he made me lobster. It was amazing." Rani learns the art of maneuvering through a kitchen from her fiancé: "He kind of introduced me into cooking and I realized it is kind of cool." Auditi also learned how to craft meals from her husband,

> I learned to cook more from [my husband]. He was always cooking, and I was more likely to be in the kitchen with him and see him cooking ... I learned the appreciation for cooking or to be comfortable with cooking and with the actual physical putting together of a meal.

My research participants not only resist the food=women=family equation, but they also go over gendered boundaries in the kitchen. The women leave the daily cooking to the men in their lives, and they also learned to prepare meals from their partners, cooking only on special occasions, like a spouse's birthday.

The women who cook prepare "one-pot" items that do not require laborious preparation. All the women whom I interviewed either have full time jobs, are full time students, or work full time and attend school part time. Due to time constraints coupled with the one-pot rule, my research participants rarely indulge in cooking "desi" or *deshi* (in Bengali, "desi" is pronounced "deshi") dishes. Rekha simply says, "I like to cook things that are self-contained. I don't like too many pots and pans. The reason I don't cook Indian food is not because I don't want to. It is just very detail oriented. You have to grind the spice and I don't really have time, frankly."

Sujata candidly expresses, "I am all about one-bowl meals. Things have to be eaten in one bowl and cooked in one pot. I make stir fries, pastas, soups, and all kinds of sandwiches ... Every now and then, I'll make Indian food just really randomly out of nowhere." Acquiring a "worldly" and "cosmopolitan" city life-style is yet another reason women choose not to curate desi food in their kitch-ens. Auditi illustrates her diverse and worldly palate:

> I do love Indian food or South Asian food in general, [but] I don't neces-sarily cook or eat Indian food at home. [My husband] loves South Asian food also. Sometimes we will go out for Indian, but most of the time it is more open. I guess that's where the New York thing comes in. I really like being very open—Thai Ethiopian and trying an amalgam of things. I try to be diverse [and] not specifically desi at all. I try to have more of a worldly experience.

Juhi has access to numerous restaurants within walking distance of her apartment:

> A couple of blocks over, there is this great Afghani place, [and] they have amazing kabobs, and that's like one of my favorites, a hole-in-the-wall place ... There are some Indian restaurants that I really like here, some Japanese ... Basically, I have a favorite in every ethnic category because that's easy to do that here.

Next, my research participants' eating habits underscore food consumption as a site of perceived assimilation. The women's daily diets consist of food items that are considered "standard American foods" like pastas, salads, soups, and sandwiches. Supriya describes salads as her go to meal,

> It is funny because when I do go to India, they are like, "What do you eat?" "I eat salad." An Indian's perception of salad is like three slices of tomato and three slices of cucumber. I have lots of lettuce [and] lots of all the vegetables that I like. That's usually what I have for dinner.

Noopur's typical diet consists of bagels, sandwiches, and pastas: "If I eat breakfast, [it's] bagels and yogurt ... Lunch, I typically prefer a sandwich and soup, like a turkey sandwich ... Dinner, I like probably more so pastas [or] maybe like a turkey burger, stuff like that. I guess typical kind of stuff." Unanimously, out-of-the-ordinary breakfast items include pancakes, waffles, and omelets. Lunch and dinner treats encompass "restaurant food" of any kind with dessert and wine. Noopur says, "Like some sort of really good omelet with like potatoes or something [for breakfast]. And then for dinner, I'd probably have to go with Thai and say there's this basil chicken dish with rice and probably a glass of wine would be great." And because the women in this study rarely create meals in their home, hot, home-cooked foods of any kind are prized. Supriya fantasizes about homemade spaghetti and *kheer* (rice pudding): "I eat in restaurants so much that it isn't a treat. Home cooking of any type is a treat for me ... Homemade apple pie or homemade *kheer* ... Homemade spaghetti is also a treat ... Someone providing me hot food is a treat." Juhi dreams about *biryani* (baked rice with lamb, chicken, or mutton): "When I go home, my mom will cook *biryani* ... [and] she will make all those kinds of foods."

My research participants describe fast-paced busy lifestyles and for no one is cooking a priority. Many eat at restaurants or get take-out, some leave food preparation to their partners, and others prepare and eat easy-to-make and easy-to-clean one-pot items. None of the women in my fieldwork consider food and cooking to be an essential part of their identity as (South Asian) women. Here, home-cooked Bengali foods are waning because women do not have the time, nor do they have the desire. The food-centered experiences also reveal that the increasing entry of women in the workforce has produced challenges to cooking in traditional ways. Thus, we see more men cooking in this study and influencing the ways in which women cook. At length, not only do my respondents reject a middle-class feminized positionality, but they also jettison the notion of an imagined South Asian woman.

5   Ethnic Chic

On a day-to-day basis, the women whom I interviewed wear what they describe as "American" clothing whether it is "standard American" or "alternative American" clothing. Priyanka says, "I wear anything from tube tops to turtle-neck sweater. My sense of style is classic clean-cut looking clothing that is very feminine." Nadia shares, "I love blazers, and I love jeans. I really like classy sexy, but not trashy ... My favorite outfit is a white tank top with stilettos and jeans with hoop earrings. I like dangly, big chandelier earrings ... and little black cocktail dresses. A little like Audrey Hepburn...." Ronica, on the other hand, is unable to see her sister's children because of her counterculture style:

> I'm not allowed to see her kids even though I'll cover my tattoos and take out a septum piercing, which is from India in the first place ... We had this conversation once where I had blue hair, and she basically said that she didn't want her kids to talk to the homeless people on the street in Boston and that I looked like them.

South Asian clothing such as saris or *shalwar kameezes* are reserved for religious-cultural events and social gatherings at the women's parents' or parents' friends' home. Rani, comfortable in khakis and a black shirt for our interview, pulls together what she would wear in various sociocultural contexts: "If there was a party at one of our American friends' houses, I would wear a dress or skirt. If it is at an Indian person's house, I wear a *shalwar kameez*. If [we] are going to the mondir [temple] ... I wear a sari or a *shalwar* ..." Anita, attired in khakis and a semi-form-fitting top for our time together, similarly shares: "If I was going out [at night], I would probably wear black pants and a kind of a hoochie top ... If I was going to an Indian wedding, obviously, Indian clothes." The sociocultural partitions clearly divide more than just space. Clothing is a wonderful example of how mental distinctions are concretized. Wearing clothes contextually helps the women to substantiate the mental distinction between "desi" and "American." In this study, my informants partition their closets into "desi" and "American" spheres to help them compartmentalize into separate cultural clusters. Women house their desi clothing in the remote parts of their closet, keeping them separate from their daily "American" wear, or they leave most of their desi clothes at their parents' homes. Ronica imparts, "Underwear and socks in one drawer ... I fold most things like pants and put them in one place, and skirts probably in a similar place, and tops in another place. My Indian clothes will have a separate place." Auditi takes a moment to mentally visualize her closet. She says, "I do have a whole other side of my closet where I have my Indian clothes—my *shalwars*, my *lehengas* ..." Differentiation of space reinforces mental differentiations (Zerubavel 1991, 7).

However, due to the neoliberal value placed on "ethnicity" in today's global fashion industry, some pieces of clothing that may have resided in the dark, hidden side of the women's closet, migrate to the popular, visible side. The neoliberal global relationship between fashion and ethnicity enables my research participants to feel comfortable and "chic" including South Asian–specific clothing and/or jewelry to their "American" outfits almost daily. Like the women in Maira's study, who sport a nose ring and *dupatta* or scarf with slinky club wear, Tina parts her lips, slightly smiling, as she expresses with pride, "I like to consider [my style] 'ethnic chic.' I like kurtas with jeans or black pants and heels ... I wear Indian jewelry with almost anything." Auditi, a woman who immediately struck me as humble, poised, and sophisticated, remarks,

> [My sense of style is] kind of a mishmash of New York/New England with a hint of desi thrown in. I tend to dress conservative mainstream. I don't wear a lot of color and gold jewelry. [But], I like to throw in something that has a fabric or something that has a desi influence.

Tina and Auditi offer how "ethnic" culture figures into their styles of daily dressing. In part, the women address a priority to assert their cultural identities in response to exclusion, but they equally show identification with "American" culture and inclusion. Noopur shares a memory of wearing a "fusiony" *shalwar kameez* at an office party:

> Typically, [I wear desi outfits at] weddings [and] Durga Pujas ... [But] I wore an Indian outfit to our [office] holiday party last year ... Well, it was an outfit that I had designed, so it was pretty like fusiony. [It] wasn't your typical like bright pink, gaudy outfit, but it was like black and gray and sleeveless, and it was almost just a two-piece outfit you see these days in [any department store].

The neoliberal global popularity of "ethnic" fashion inspires my research participants to bring certain items, such as a *dupatta*, to high traffic areas of their closets. The clothing practices presented here are peculiarly cosmopolitan and refer to middle- to upper-middle-class women who possess cultural capital and participate in bourgeois consumption patterns. The terms of participation within clothing practices are, furthermore, situated in the contingent contextuality of the spaces and places in which the women are in. Raghuram (2003) writes, "... wearing clothing requires a sensitivity not simply to ethnicity, or to class and gender, but also to spatially situated racialized codes" (79). The women recognize the importance of clothes to a self-definition of South Asian, American, and South Asian American.

The hybrid fashion consumption tales I share here are not entirely untroubled. While indeed the women confidently reconfigure what it means to American, they are also solidifying racialized capitalism.[2] Raghuram (2003)

---

2 My focus on consumption is an attempt is to overturn the economic determinism of production studies models and to recognize the spatial-temporal contingency of the products and processes. In other words, I study meanings without posting those meanings as universal.

writes, the "local embeddedness of retailing is accompanied by a more global embeddedness in production linkages that have been facilitated by a longer-standing social relations" (68). In other words, the global popularity of hybrid-ethnic fashions enables the women to express (brown) culture without being marked as the Other, and this speaks to class formation. Globalization is predominantly theorized in terms of social openness and social fluidity but a small social stratus of "cosmocrats" live the reality of hypermobility (Shamir 2005, 188). Raghuram (2003) breaks open the ways in which working class South Asian American women are unable to participate in hybrid-ethnic consumption: Working class women are bound to clothing that was brought with them from the "homeland" years ago—now dated in any fashion context—or they sew garments (73). U.S.-based model-minority class (and citizenship) privileges manifest racialized gender constructions (often in generational contexts): the ugly, working-class South Asian woman and the chic, South Asian woman, or *Masala-itis* (Dasgupta 1993). According to Puar (1994b), "The stereotype of the dirty, ugly South Asian woman thus becomes exoticized through middle-class consumption" (37). Ronica is apt here,

> The privilege to be able to come and go from India is a big deal. That's very much a product of living in the Global South and having these economic realities ... There is a big difference between somebody and me who doesn't have an American passport in terms of what my privilege is in the world ... Later migrations don't have that same privilege.

Differential ability to move in space is a major stratifying force in the global social hierarchy (Shamir 2005, 200).

In closing the discussion on clothing, fashion is dynamic and has a historical dimension to it. The clothing practices of the second-generation South Asian American women or "diasporic youth" not only produces a situated reading of "diaspora" as a localized cultural form (Mani 2003, 117), but it also shows that crossing lines that mark off perceived insular chunks of space serve to articulate passage through mental partitions (Zerubavel 1991, 7). Noopur's "fusiony" fashion sense, Tina's "ethnic chic" style, and Auditi's need to put a little "desi kick" into her appearance hint at diasporic formation that includes privileging hybridity, and hybridity offers a sense of "home" along with a call of authenticity for the second-generation (Puar 1994b, 103). But the hybrid-ethnic approaches in formulating the South Asian Diaspora effaces the significance of certain pieces of clothing and even histories behind why particular ingredients are used in cooking (Narayan 1997, 159–88), obliterating the fact that the two "origins" of the hybrid are by no means equal. Naber (2006) argues that hybridity "fails to account for the ways that essentialist categories, while constructed and fictive, operate to support hierarchies of privilege and domination and power and control" (108). Raghuram (2003) comments on the commodification process involved in producing authenticity: "Along with the status value, there is also a symbolic value to the clothes they wear, which arises out of the meaning-making processes formed within reference systems bounded by class differences but also racialized and gendered differences" (76). Hybrid-ethnic or diasporic clothing not only rests on hegemonic notions of capital, but it also generates out of a history of clothing practices that denote both colonial and nationalist attempts to represent the nation (Mani 2003, 121).

I do not wish to efface the specificities of race and gender and my respondents acts of deliberate resistance. Puar (1994b) argues hybridity serves as a powerful and positive tool for the second generation. The women with whom I worked counter gendered and racialized notions of the body and they disrupt the tradition-modernity binary, problematizing "the paradigmatic constructions of the referent geopolitical entities" (Raghuram 2003, 69–70). By "mixing and matching," the women subvert the stereotypical South Asian woman, altering the meanings of the clothes they purchase and wear (Raghuram 2003). The women, collectively, counter celebrations of essentialist thinking of ethnicity by focusing on the "hybrid" (Bhabha 1990; Gilroy 1995) and rupture the oppositional discourse behind tradition and modernity. Escoffier writes (1991), "One major limitation of identity politics and its representation in multiculturalism is that we are all born within a web of overlapping identities and group affiliations" (64) and Minh-Ha (1989) says, "Despite our desperate, eternal attempt to separate, contain, and mend, categories always leak" (94). The exploration uncovers the paradoxes of class, gender, and racial formations in the United States, and what emerges from the data is how my respondents interact with their identities as South Asian American women. The women's expressions of cultural practices through the five territories of the self underscore the agency they have in asserting, enhancing, maintaining, and reconstructing their identities. Clothing choices among the second-generation South Asian American women are distinctly political acts that both disturb the assumed coherence between categories of race, nation, and culture and reaffirm essentialized identities (Mani 2003). The women I interviewed reject the hegemonic conception of a unitary self.

CHAPTER 7

Project of "Home"

"Where Are You From?"

"I always get asked, 'Where are you from?' And, if I don't give the *right* answer, then I get, 'No, what I mean is, where are you *really* from?'" Sunita shares haunting words with me. As a second-generation Bangladeshi American woman, born to and raised by immigrant parents in the United States, I conceptualized this chapter from a personal self-project (Spivak 1988; hooks 1990; Puar 1994a), one that stemmed from not being able to coherently articulate the answer to the question, "Where are you from?" I have come to realize that I am not the only one to struggle to answer the question of home satisfactorily. Mohanty (1993) offers a personal story about flying back to the United States after participating in an academic conference in the Netherlands: "On a TWA flight ... the professional white man sitting next to me asks: a) which school do I go to? And b) when do I plan to go home?—all in the same breath ..." (351). The "Other" narrative is legitimized and enforced by the question "Where are you from? ... Where are you *really* from?" Visweswaran (1993) shares,

> Certainly, the question, "Where are you from?" is never an innocent one. Yet not all subjects have equal difficulty in replying. To pose a question of origin is subtly to pose a question of return, to challenge not only temporally, but geographically, one's place in the present ... it is a question which provokes a sudden failure of confidence, the fear of never replying adequately. (301)

Puar (1994a) argues the reason we struggle is because it is the question that is problematic, not the answer. The question becomes exclusionary and racist: the purpose is to remind us that we neither belong here nor fit in.

Monolithic or "linear notions of home" refer to the naturalized, apparently self-evident qualities that are attached to the idea of "home" (Gillis 1997). Most multicultural models assume assimilation as the benchmark and often link "home" to a single spatial location. The question "Where are you from?" is embedded in the construction of home as a "situated, fixed, safe sphere, with ties to place." Mohanty (1993) extends her story:

I have been asked the "home" question (when are you going home) peri-
odically for fifteen years now. Leaving aside the subtly racist implications of the question (go home—you don't belong here), I am still not
satisfied with my response. What is home? ... I am convinced that this
question—how one understands and defines home—is a profoundly
political one. (352)

As a Professor of Sociology, Women and Gender Studies, and Critical Race and
Ethnicity Studies, I am particularly concerned about thinking through diverse
languages, images, myths, and rituals through which home is represented and
constituted. Gillis (1997) insists that non-linear notions of home have an existence independent of actual living arrangements. Here, "home" is a mental
construct that is no less real than the household itself and I argue it is constituted through a set of cultural practices. Grappling with the psychological
impact of encountering the question "Where are you from?" (Puar 1994a, 21),
I think through U.S. racial projects and the notion of "home" in this chapter.

1   "Where Are You *Really* From?"

Unanimously, my research participants are queried where they are from in a
multitude of social contexts. Visweswaran (1993) considers Vrudhula's poem,
entitled "Do not belong to this or that, but I am here":

Are you from India?
No, my parents are.
Oh, How exciting! You know I saw the movie Gandhi, I thought it was
    great ... Have you been?
Oh, yes, of course!
(I've only gone once, I was already 23)
The guy I work with is from India. You must know him? His name, uh ...
    let me think, oh yes, Patel? (306)

Vrudhula conveys the ignorance with which most Americans view South Asia
(specifically referencing India). She expresses how second-generation South
Asian Americans handle the presumption that they are not from here, i.e., the
U.S., and Vrudhula's lack of response to the question of home reflects the nature
of the question, a denial that Vrudhula and other South Asian Americans are
from here (and there and everywhere). The tacit assumption behind the question of home is one of Orientalist foreignness. Juhi explains she is often asked

where she is from because people find it tough to categorize her phenotypic characteristics within available U.S. racial and ethnic structures, rendering Juhi as "exotic":

> [I remember being] at a St. Patrick's Day party with my friends. They were all white, [and] this one guy says, "My friend and I have been staring at you for the past half hour wondering what you are." I wanted to punch the guy, so I said, "What do you think I am?" He literally guessed fifteen different things. ...

Grewal contends hegemonic discourses of this nation use racist images of minority groups as a formative structure of citizenship (70). Racist images are absorbed into economics, racialized structures of the nation-state, U.S. imperial history and militarism, and the globalization of capital and labor. Plainly, the question of home, first, is prompted by the ambiguous ways in which race is defined in the United States, and second, the question of home is embedded in the genealogy of U.S. and "western" colonization (situated in a discourse that ties home to a single space). Juhi understands the racialized link between the question of home and what it means to be a normative American (read as "white"). She angrily engages in claim-staking American nation-state borders via birth/citizenship and education/profession/class or what I call "points of assimilation,"

> I am American. I am just as American as you are because I was born in this country. Maybe my parents weren't born in this country, but I grew up here. Maybe some of [my experiences] were different but I've had a lot of the same experiences as you. I went to the same type of school and college, and I work in the same type of job.

The women in my research are clear that as South Asians in America, they are positioned within essentialist categories that operate and support hierarchies of privilege, domination, power, and control.

When asked the home question, Rupa, at times, works within a bifurcated boundary—South Asian versus American—by explaining her parents' immigration from Bangladesh to the U.S. and her location in the assimilation model as an ABCD or a South Asian who is U.S.-born. On most occasions, however, she firmly redraws the boundary by simply stating that she is from upstate New York. Rupa says, "I might take the time of giving them the complicated answer, 'I was born and raised here, and my parents are from blah blah.' But mostly I'll say, 'Logan Square,' and that is it. ..." Rupa problematizes the home question and shares a story with me about racialized identity work, transnational travels and im/migration, and the notion of home:

> I have a girlfriend who just went back to Taiwan within the past week, and she wrote me this story over the e-mail about how she was sitting in a Chinese language class and the teacher asked her in Chinese, "Where did you come from?" She did not know how to answer so the teacher thought she was stupid. "Does that mean am I from Taiwan, or am I from Chicago, or am I from New York?"

Auditi shares, "If I am traveling in India ... invariably the question is, 'Where are you from?' I say that 'I am American,' and they say, 'No, you're not American.'" Puar (1994b) provide a wonderful backdrop in which to situate the women's stories. She writes,

> Immigration is not a one-time movement; it is a complex shifting of localities of physical and emotional states, which begins way before and extends far beyond the actual event. As children of immigrants, we are denied these realities by western society, yet constantly reminded of them. The actuality and validity of our displaced, "outsider" identities is hence negated. Why else should this question be asked? (22)

Foucault (1990; 1994; 1995) aptly rejects the idea of knowledge, truth, and language as neutral, arguing that knowledge is always connected to power: (Modern) discourses that formalize knowledge regulate and control our experiences. At the heels of Rupa's experiences, Jhumpa expresses, "When someone asks me where I am from ... it really makes me antsy because I know what they are trying to get at. But I will just be like, 'oh, I am from L.A.'" To both work within and redraw the fictive and constructed boundaries between South Asian and American, Laila, asks for clarification before responding to the question of home: "I always ask an explanation question, 'Do you mean where my family is from or where I grew up?' I don't know if they want to know if I am from Virginia or if they want to know my ethnicity or if they want to know if I was born in this country." My informants, like Rupa's friend, are denied multiple alliances and multiple homes that may even be contradictory.

My research participants continue to stress experiences of national unbelonging by sharing stories with me about being interrogated by brown folk or other South Asians. Priyanka talks to me about one of her train rides into Manhattan:

One morning an Indian man got on, and he sat right next to me. He finally decided to say something. First, he asked me if I was Indian, which is the standard first question ... He [then] asked me if I spoke Hindi ... After all that, he asked me, "So, how long have you been in this country?"

While Priyanka's "foreignness" remains underscored, my informants voice they find the brown voyeur to be less oppressive. Jhumpa says,

I feel like it is more innocent in a way. I feel really guarded when white people ask me that question. I don't get as guarded when people of color, especially South Asians, ask me that question. They want to know as much as I want to know, because if I do meet someone else that is Bengali, I am like really, I am Bengali too, and there is a connection there.

Rupa says, "White men [bother me the most, but] if somebody is really nice and it is an elder, I will ask them what they mean...." Indira expresses, "I was asked that a lot in college by South Asians or even when I went to India because I don't look Bengali enough." And Juhi says, "[If] ... I am in a situation where I would meet other South Asians, it doesn't bother me as much." Bashi (1998) is illuminates the women's responses:

It makes a difference who is doing the categorical defining, and who is policing the boundaries of these definitions. It comes down to a question of power: who holds it, where the power- holders see themselves and others in the existing hierarchy, where they think they should be in the racial hierarchy ... and how they use their power to realize those norms. (965)

My respondents show that in matters of racial and ethnic identity, the person doing the identifying is consequential.

Indeed, race and ethnicity are a matter of structure and power—which racial categories and ethnicities are available for sorting, and who gets to do the sorting (Nagel 2003, 42). While citizenship privilege provides the women with some invincibility, their freedom is comprised because along with mobility, it also includes Otherness. Such are the monolithic, unmarked, and normative understandings of an American nationalist self.

2   Mobile Diasporas

The configuration of home is staged as a "situated, fixed, safe sphere, with ties to place" (Puar 1994a. 75), but my informants show me that "home" must be written as ideologically constructed, not only across space but also through time. I understand this to mean home is constituted through a set of cultural practices.

Ronica brings to life the floating and transnational nature of home by swiftly challenging the linear teleology that often accompanies the discussion of home:

> I feel strongly that if I try to create my identity here [U.S.], ignoring South Asia and my relationship to South Asia, it will totally make me feel like I was missing out, and it would make feel like I didn't have a real place in the world. In the sense of transnational, I feel real committed to going back to South Asia as often as I can and doing things there by giving back to a community that my family benefited from ... When I go to India it is very much about sharing the privilege that I have [from being an American].

Ronica comments on how post-1965 migration from South Asia, unlike Punjabi migration to California in the 1800s, eventually carried citizenship rights for many. The discourse of citizenship (and class privilege) has profound effects on the construction of home for immigrants, their children, and subsequent generations: (American) citizenship produces transnational mobile bodies. Puar (1994b) reflects, "I clutched on to [my passport] as proof of my right to movement, seeing the American eagle on its front as a sign of democracy, the freedom to move—the façade of citizenship" (87). Ronica is a "shifting and multiply positioned" subject (with the privilege of class and nation), resulting in a notion of diaspora that can no longer use a "linear teleology" home. Rupa also accentuates the complexities involved in defining her sense of home within a linear teleology:

> Right after the [Bush–Gore] elections, I wrote this really depressing poem ... One of the things I wrote was, how do I call this my land when it is practically an accident that I am even here? My dad could have gotten residency in Canada or in the U.K., but I ended up here. What are my ties here really? What does it mean to be Bengali or Muslim, growing up in this little shit town on [the East Coast]? Bangladesh, what does it mean that I call it "back home?"

Rupa demonstrates that "home" cannot be written as "one fixed place nor as a safe place, and movement is not only mobility but it [is] also about displacement" (Puar 1994a, 76). Rupa suggests dissatisfaction with a fixed and immobile conceptualization of "home." But Rupa also underscores a shifting and multiply positioned diaspora "functions as a threat to certain homes while becoming the construct of home for certain Others": It is neither a "natural" space, nor is it nation-friendly (Puar 1994a, 76–77). Rupa vocalizes the physical and sexual imagery that accompanies what it means to be both an American woman and a Bangladeshi woman, standards of femininity she is far from:

> The last time I went to Bangladesh, I remember on Eid, I was decked out … in a sari and my cousin put her wedding jewelry all over me … We took rickshaws to another khala's [maternal aunt] house … and on the way all the men in the street were coming up to the rickshaw and leering in my face, [asking], "Cheley na mey?" [Boy or girl?] and they were mean.

Like Polanyi's (1944) "double movement," Rupa's traveling is about privilege, but it is certainly not about freedom.[1] Diasporic subjects like Rupa engage with struggles in "both homes."

Tina breaks down monolithic and linear notions of "home" by questioning the meaning of "authentic" cultural expression. Tina describes her trepidation with joining Indian students' groups and associations in college: "They [foreign students from India] came here to do their undergraduate or graduate work … They thought of us as fake Indians, not authentic.…" The call for authenticity suggests "it is the 'real' immigrant who can address the 'mother country' as home and exist as its cultural authority in the West" (Puar 1994a, 100). Alternatively, unlike Tina, Rekha voices that she is not an "authentic" Indian. Rekha's training in *kathak*, a North Indian form of classical dancing, had little to do with devotion to the art of dancing. Rather, her dance practices and recitals were about socializing in her Bengali American community in the Midwest:

---

1   Like Polanyi (1944), Bhabha (1994) points to a "double narrative movement" in the construction of the nation-space and the "people." He writes, "The people are the historical 'objects' of nationalist pedagogy, giving the discourse an authority that is based on the pre-given or constituted historical origin in the past; the people are also the 'subjects' of a process of signification that must erase any prior originary presence of the nation-people to demonstrate the prodigious, living principles of the people as contemporaneity: as the sign of the present through which the national life is redeemed and iterates as a reproductive process" (209).

When I went to India, I saw what a real Indian was like—what it meant to be Indian in India. Here [America], I am going around doing this Indian dance and I look Indian ... It [dancing] was about the social network I had myself entrenched in, which was going to parties and functions. That seemed to me almost fabricated and, most importantly, I felt like I couldn't truly represent what that [kathak] really was ... I am not one of those people in India. I couldn't ever truly represent that.

The women volley in their construction of what it means be a "South Asian" and what it means to be an "American," and cultivate experiences of "discovering" an "authentic self" that are problematic (Puar 1994a, 84). Bhabha (1994) provides an impressive context in which to embed the collective experiences of my participants:

The problematic enunciation of cultural difference becomes, in the discourse of relativism, the perspectival problem of temporal and spatial distance. The threatened "loss" of meaningfulness in cross-cultural interpretation, which is as much a problem of the structure of the signifier as it is a question of cultural codes (the experience of other cultures), then becomes a hermeneutic project for the restoration of cultural "essence" of authenticity. (179)

The "authentic," therefore, seems to be an amorphous and constantly shifting figure, "depending on geopolitical locations and categories, constructing the mutually exclusive either/or nature of the paradigmatic figure" (Puar 1994a, 84).

Finally, Tina's travels to Calcutta are captured by the legacy of the white traveler on vacation—luxury, leisure, and privilege: "People take us for granted. They think that dollars grow on trees. Every time we go back, it is assumed that we are going to treat them just because we are from the U.S." Noopur observes, "My [family in India] make comments that we have everything ... Outside of America, [life] is made out to look like we snap our fingers, and five hundred dollars falls into my lap." Ronica says,

When I am in Calcutta ... It is so embarrassing to be totally singled out and treated like you are a prima donna ... What's embarrassing about that is knowing that I haven't done anything to receive that privilege or to receive that recognition [except] be born in another country.

Mohanty (1993) writes, "Notions of home and community are located within a deeply political space, where racialization and gender and class relations and histories become the prism through which [to understand], however partially, what it could mean to be South Asian in North America ... [and] the meanings attached to home and community in India" (353).

At length, my research participants' oral histories suggest they produce a complex process of identity within U.S. racial and ethnic structures and trans-nationalism: South Asia and America are "home and "not-home." Mankekar (1994) foregrounds the ability of diasporic subjects to engage with struggles in "both our 'homes'" (351). She focuses on "cultural bifocality" to acknowledge the engagements, connections, and continuities between "discontinuous spaces," and she emphasizes continuities and connections to make room for diasporic stories that are not about loss or starting anew. Drawing on Mankekar, I argue the women's experiences of what I call the "project of home(s)" is a product of considerable effort and agency and is a reassertion of their identity as South Asian American women—an act of choice in the face of constraints—rather than passive conformity with (trans)national traditions. The women involved in my fieldwork speak to their struggles in defining "home," articulating their identities within a constellation of intersecting loyalties that are multiple, contradictory, shifting, and overlapping. My informants' herstories are class-, race-, and gender-specific negotiations of the transnational experience of crafting a South Asian American identity.

CHAPTER 8

Cultural Autonomy

Boundaries of Marriage

Heterosexual ethnoreligious endogamous marriage is a key demand of South Asian (American) womanhood. The women's stories reveal that marriage constitutes the yardstick for policing female subjectivities (in cultural nationalist terms). In this chapter, I focus on the role marriage plays in my research participants' lives: I explore how the women respond to their families' expectations of marriage coupled with the women's expectations of marriage. By searching the transcripts, I discover the women in my fieldwork frame their tales of marital heteronormativity within three ideal types: the "suitable boy" or the "ideal" husband, the "ideal" age, and "ideal" cultural endogamy. The women report a familial imagination of the "ideal husband": families expect their daughters to marry men who fall into the families' parameters of acceptability. Here, the women voice that their families and community members demand them to play the role of carriers of (desi American national) culture. Next, my participants articulate to fulfill their families' expectations of marriage and to attract the ideal mate, they must enter the "marriage market" and pursue potential partners while in their twenties. I learn that with age, it becomes less and lease feasible for the women to fulfill the imagined idealized South Asian American daughterhood. Finally, while my respondents feel coercive familial pressure to marry, the women themselves reproduce idealized diasporic selfhood. Collectively, the women indicate they are unwilling to marry outside of "their" culture. They express a longing for an intimate partnership in which they are not required to explain their ethnocultural traditions. Surprisingly, I find my respondents do not ignore the histories and nuances of the practice of arranged marriage; arranged marriages in the second-generation community are not uncommon. Here, my research participants map falling in love as a modern American technology and, hence, the women re-engineer the arranged marriage by decentering the stigmas (strict, inflexible, and patriarchal) that come along with arranged marriage. Taken together, the women in this study interpret the regulatory ideals of marriage as the central feature that renders them embraceable within their families and community as ideal South Asian women and daughters in America.

1   Suitable Boy (Feminized Cultural Carriers)

The fear of daughters dating—there is little attempt to control men's (hetero-) sexuality—consumes many South Asian families; daughters are frequently policed with the stick of tradition and called on to preserve national culture (Mani 1993, 34–35). My respondents report their families (and desi community members) closely guard their sexualities and both parents are complicit and vested in their daughters' prospects of marriage. The women narrate stories about how their mothers and fathers and fictive aunts and uncles (and at times older siblings)—South Asian cultural authorities in America—sew together the meaning of the ideal marriage. The ideal marriage is decorated with immigrant nostalgia, imagined "true" South Asianness, the myth of the model-minority, and gendered labor and fashioned by marrying within one's religious group, economic class, national group, and racialized ethnic group. I find the categories are (somewhat) hierarchical: religious affiliation (Muslim or Hindu, including caste for Hindu families) supersedes economic class (model minority myth), economic class supersedes national origin (Bangladeshi or Indian), and national origin supersedes racialized ethnic identity (Bengali).[1]

    Auditi's family expected her to select a husband from an endogamous "kin" group—"their kind"—fashioned through religion, nationality, and racialized ethnic group:

> [My parents'] biggest concern is a Bengali Brahman—somebody whose family speaks the same language and not just the literal language, but also all of it—the cultural language, the framework, and all of that ... The interest is having this real similar cultural, basically being able to replicate what they had had ... Somebody with whom I would carry on the religious and cultural traditions, and we would raise children who would also speak fluent Bengali, and we would all go to puja together ... [My mom] really expected [me] to follow the Bengali woman ways.

Rani's Bengali Brahman mother communicated disdain toward Rani's Christian Malayalam fiancé:

> My mother says, "Oil and water do not mix ... Look at what they are getting and what we are getting?" She will say it flat out ... It should be somebody who is fair, good-looking, a doctor, Bengali Brahman, and speaks the

---

1   Caste is a status system and a form of social closure (Aneesh and Borocz 2000).

language ... It should definitely [be] somebody who is going to be able to take care of me financially ... Our parents are so scared. They want us to marry the same thing so that we can carry on our culture throughout the generations.

Within heteronormative endogamy, some women described an acceptable alternative: a non-Bengali South Asian man from the appropriate religion. Rani says, "Now [my mom] has opened up to at least that they don't need to be Bengali, but they need to be Brahman. She tells me, 'It is your birthright!'" Rupa shares, "[My parents] don't care if he is from [Bangladesh] or Pakistan or India, but he must be Muslim. That was what I grew up with. I always struggled against that, but I thought if he wasn't, he will convert." Zerubavel (1991) insights are helpful here. People carve reality into discrete mental slices, "islands of meaning," which they categorize, classify, and label. We structure our lives into territories, partitions, and classes. The experiential of discrete entities presumes a perception of boundaries surrounding us, and such "fine lines" lead us to perceive a fundamental discontinuity between insiders and outsiders, "those included in a social cluster and those who are left outside its confines" (14). Only in relation to such lines, the women in this study learn who is available to them as a sexual partner and whom they must avoid. Unanimously, my respondents reveal that Hindu men for Muslim women and Muslim men for Hindu women are outside the prescribed boundaries of marriageability. My research participants' disclosures expose that the categorical boundaries are to be protected by a daughter's marriage and the production of "ideal" children.

Yegenoglu (1998) specifically asserts brown women's bodies are a symbol of tradition, and, thus, they are often "used to represent national identity or ethnic loyalty" (Maira 2002, 14). The women in this study emerge as the bearers of tradition and they are expected to reproduce "South Asia" in the home (and be responsible for preventing acculturation of the children). The discourse of an imagined "true" South Asian culture re- produces a cultural nationalist logic that is predicated on the idea that an imagined South Asian community loses itself to "Americanization" if a daughter chooses to betray the regulatory demands of an idealized South Asian American womanhood (Naber 2006, 92). The significance of the current discussion is that my research participants are the carriers of (national) culture as South Asian American women.

2   "How Old Is Your Daughter?" (Masculinist Cultural Production)

As part of the regulatory demands of an idealized South Asian womanhood, the women account pressure from their families to be married (and have children) before they reach thirty. Juhi's mother is strict about when a woman should be married:

> My mom point blank told me I had to be married when I was twenty-five. And she's like, "I am not playing around." I didn't even know how to react to that because she was so dead set about that. She was like, "You have to start your family. This is ridiculous now. I was twenty-two when I got married."

Noopur similarly relays,

> For some reason, with [my parents], it's like this set pattern of life: You go to school until you're 22, you work until you're 25, [and] you get married and start having kids before you're 30. It's like bam, bam, bam.

Both Juhi and Noopur's testimonies expel mid-twenties is the ideal time for a South Asian American woman to be married. Noopur clarifies that by then, a woman has presumably graduated from college and gained some work experience and that means women are ready to take their appropriate place in the community as responsible daughters, i.e., marital accessibility.

I find the parental culturally mandated age bar is often motivated by virginal primacy or the families' fears about their daughters' sexuality or symbolic pollution/contamination. In addition, I unearth that "too much" education and employment are not valuable attributes and must be curbed. Rita says, "I'm going to go out to work and I'm going to become independent, which is such a bad word for our parents for some reason. So, then they were, 'When are you going to get married?'" Extended educational training, like pursuing a graduate or professional degree, "buys" the daughters time from the demands of South Asian American womanhood. Rita explains the next point of entry into marriage is after graduate training (presumably women are in their late twenties):

> I think the worst [my parents] got was when I was twenty-three [after I graduated college]. [But] when I started law school, it wasn't that bad because I was so extremely busy and whenever they would say anything, I would say, I can't think about that. The second year, they are looking at graduation—again, they were like, "When are you going to get married?"

Juhi speaks of a related pressure, "Ideally, I think [my mother] would like me
to be married now, but I told her that because of my masters there is just no
way it is going to happen in the next two years. Then her next thing is, 'When
you're done, then it's just going to happen.'" My research participants advise me
that once women are in their thirties, higher education is no longer an appropriate reason to abstain from marriage. Anjana, a doctoral candidate, speaks
about the value of her marriage in her parents' lives: "[My parents] keep saying,
'Do you really want to do this school thing? What's so bad about just getting
married now?' So, they really want me to just get married and have kids right
away, and the school thing should be on the back burner." Noopur intimates
her parents' expectations of her older sister's marriage, "With my sister, [my
parents are] starting to get a little nervous ... The fact that she's approaching
30 and could strike 30 and that she's not going to have those kids at 30, it kind
of throws them for a loop...." The women in this study translate the meaning of being thirty and over: old, less beautiful, and a diminished capacity to
bear children. In this context, the women's families are less steadfast about
whom their daughters should marry—excluding taboo populations—if the
women are married. Mazeda reviews how the familial accepted circle of partners widens when South Asian American daughters "age out": "[My parents]
want me to get married and have kids. So, part of me is thinking that pretty
much anyone I bring home by the time I am thirty years old (unless they're
Black)." In overriding the ethno-religious ideal with the heterosexual imperative, my respondents' parents reinforce control over the conjugal heterosexual
and family ideals over their daughters in the South Asian American national
context (Naber 2006, 102). The testimonies crack open that the women have a
small window of what I name as "marriage marketability," or marital access to
men from within one's own religious group, economic class, national group,
and racialized ethnic group.

3   (Un)Suitable Boy (Changing Contours of Boundaries)

Mazeda' critical communication reflects the changing contours of religious,
economic, national group, and racial and ethnic boundaries for South Asian
Americans. By further searching through the transcripts for thin references to
descriptions of intimate partnerships, I find the forging of an imagined South
Asian identity in America through ethnoreligious endogamy unravels. The
meaning of marrying from an endogamous "kin" group or "their kind" is complex. First, while the regulatory demands of South Asian American womanhood are framed as an alternative to U.S. assimilation, the cultural discourse

controlling a daughter's marriageability activates a family strategy of American assimilation. And second, the Orientalist South Asian/American binary shifts in accordance with power relations à la U.S. racialized and classed immigration structure that set the stage for expressing and/or transgressing idealized South Asian American femininity, including the availability of adequate exogamous partners.

Collectively, the women expose their refusal to form intimate partnerships with South Asian men who are FOBs or "bananas." Nadia provides a telling testimony, "I would never date a FOB and I would never marry one. There is a reason for it: They are backwards!" Nandita feels she needs to be with someone who grew up with *Gilligan's Island*:

> One of the things that I think of a lot, and it's a joke among my friends, is I need my husband to know who Gilligan is. That's kind of how I foresee the difference of someone who's brought up and grown up here and has the same background and the same thought processes as I do. When they see that red shirt, they should go, "Oh, my gosh, that's Gilligan!"

Juhi says, "I think ideally I would like someone who was Bangladeshi *but* grew up here and who obviously comes from a professional and economically stable family...." The Orientalist "foreignness" of immigrant South Asian men or FOBs/bananas reflect the instability of an imagined "true" South Asian culture. Nadia, Nandita, and Juhi speak to their placement in U.S. racialized and classed immigration structure and their imagination of a "suitable boy" disrupts the women's homogenous South Asian world. Next, Padmini and Laila discover the acceptability of exogamous partners—"white" men. Padmini, a Hindu woman, says:

> I was dating this Jewish guy for a while. [My parents] were very enthusiastic about that, but it didn't pan out. I guess it is the stereotypical thing that you hear that white is much more acceptable at least than a black person. This is totally not to offend you, but a friend of ours, she is marrying a Bangladeshi Muslim, and my mother recently said that even a white person would be better than that.

Laila, a Muslim, voices,

> I think [both Black and Hindu] would matter more than a Christian or a Jew. [My parents] have talked about me and who I should be with. My

dad has basically said that he wouldn't really be happy to see me with a
Hindu guy.

As part of the South Asian American matrix of femininity and sexuality, marriage and having children are on the forefront of Ronica's family discussions
also, especially as Ronica approaches thirty. Ronica's parents have expressed
on several occasions they would even approve of a white man, though not a
Muslim, at this point: "It is interesting now because I think they are starting
to get desperate. They are like, 'You can even marry a white man.' I am like,
'Mmmm, that's nice.' They want me to get married. They would like for him
to be white or South Asian and not Muslim." In learning of a Muslim man's
unsuitability, Ronica comes to terms with the heterogeneity of South Asian
American cultural identity. Ronica self-identifies as gender queer and in the
context of Ronica's queer identity, the heterosexual imperative becomes a
deeper significant symbol of the South Asian/American boundary than the
"virginity" ideal. Anzaldúa (2001) writes, "For the lesbian of color, the ultimate
rebellion she can make against her native culture is through her sexual behavior. She goes against two moral prohibitions: sexuality and homosexuality" (17).
Ronica's queerness underwrites her marginalization as traitor-American to her
cultural authoritative desi parents. In overriding the virginity ideal with the
heterosexual imperative, Ronica's parents reinforce control over female sexuality that underlie the heterosexual conjugal ideal in both South Asian and
American national cultures. Yet, when Ronica's parents replace the marriage
taboo around whiteness with Muslim, they reveal the gaps and fissures within
the idea of a unified South Asian nationalist identity and the ways in which an
imagined "true" South Asian culture shifts depending on sociohistorical circumstances. Indeed, fissures in an imagined "authentic" or "true" South Asian
culture emerge when the women's parents suggest that they bring home "even
a white man." The complexities of "suitable boys" among the women and their
families reveal the difficulties of applying any single model of identity.

4   "I Don't Want to Have to Explain Everything about Myself!"

The women in this study begin to recognize the heterogeneity of South Asian
American cultural identity, while they remain committed to reproducing idealized notions of diasporic selfhood. Collectively, my respondents' practice cultural autonomy—a vital theme in this book. Many of the women I interviewed
are unwilling to marry outside of "their culture" not only because they long
for a sense of cultural commonality, but also because it honors their parents'

stories of im/migration of struggle. The women interpret the regulatory ideals of marriage as the most salient feature of familial and communal embraceability. Tonima says she would not consider marrying outside of her South Asian Muslim community because it would be difficult for her Bangladeshi Muslim parents to come to terms with:

> [My parents] would freak out [if I brought home a Black or Hindu], and then I think they would accept it at some time or another just because they are my parents. But I know I would have to have gone through hell. I don't want to go through that. I don't feel like it is worth it. I don't think I could go out with someone who is non-desi.

Juhi chooses desi cultural commonality because she does not want to explain herself:

> There are certain jokes that another South Asian person will understand that a white person just won't get. I think where I am at in my life and the way that I want to be, I don't want to have to deal with, "Oh what does that mean?" I have had to do that before, and I just don't want to deal with it.

Rupa expresses reasons like Juhi:

> [In college,] if I would cook something and eat with my hands, [my boyfriend] would say, "If you did that at my mother's table, we would have to call you a savage." Shit like that ... I don't want to have to explain everything about myself and about my culture and what I mean by this. It is exhausting ... I don't think I would want that in my life.

Next, the women in my study who align with exogamous partners (outside of the endogamous circle but not entirely taboo) find ways to maintain their diasporic cultural connectedness. Auditi and Noopur profess their sexual attraction to white men and since both women remain deeply vested in their Bengali Hindu culture, they seek out white men who are open to learning about and participating in the women's traditions and customs. Noopur says,

> Being that my preference is probably non-Indian ... I need someone that is adaptable to my culture. My culture is a huge part of me. I am not saying that I need someone who will convert to Hinduism. What I mean is more someone that is willing to learn and at least adapt partially.

And Auditi declares:

> My relationship with my family and my relatives and culture are import-
> ant to me, and to be able to go to a puja or my cousin's wedding and get
> dressed up, and eat the food, and do that unquestioningly, and having
> a partner that is willing to do that or at least be interested in it ... [My
> husband] is more Indian than we are. He is not, but he fits in so well, and
> I realize on some level I knew that's what I was going to be most com-
> fortable with. I was lucky, but it wasn't that it just accidentally happened.

Noopur describes a short-term love interest. What caught her attention was
that he knew she was Bengali:

> I met him through friends through work, and we had hit it off. The
> first thing he had said to me—and this goes back to one of the biggest
> things that I look for in men—was something about the fact that I hap-
> pen to be Bengali. He's straight-up Midwestern, Caucasian guy, and so it
> impressed me.

Auditi and Noopur problematize the idea that "brown" women who are in
interracial relationships are rebels and symbols of final U.S. assimilation (Puar
1994a). On the contrary, the women challenge assimilationist beliefs about
interracial relationships, which presume differences between two cultures to
be so great that the "Other" culture must submit to the dominant or the privileging of whiteness (Puar 1994a). Simply put, Auditi and Noopur refuse to play
the "Masala-itis" role (Dasgupta 1993; Puar 1994b).

Finally, two women—Indira and Jhumpa—form intimate alliances with
men who are "taboo." While the terms of South Asianness are constructed on
communalist tendencies among South Asians in America and their distinction from Blackness, Indira and Jhumpa are in intimate relationships outside
the brown–white matrix, forming romantic and marriage alliances outside the
brown/white continuum. Indira unearths the history of Asian-Black alliance
in the U.S. (Prashad 2002) through her personal history. Indira is married to
a bi-racial Black man from a single-parent and working-class household. And
Jhumpa resurrects the lost history of Punjabi-Mexican alliances (Leonard
1997): she is dating a Mexican American man from a working-class family.
While Indira and Jhumpa reject practices of oppositionally active whiteness
and strategic assimilation, the women are not oblivious to being on the on the
"wrong" side of the culture/class line. Indira says it was easy to date her husband because he does not "look Black":

He is mixed. His mother is Black, and his father was white. He doesn't look like anything distinct. A lot of people think he is Indian because he is about my color. He is kind of light ... I don't think the concept [of him being Black] sank in [with my parents] because he is my color, and he doesn't look Black.

Jhumpa struggled for months thinking about whether she should pursue a long-term relationship with a Mexican man, and when she decided to date her partner, she found that she was unable to tell her mother about him for over two years:

I am twenty-five years old, and I should be able to tell my parents who I am dating. What if we do take it to another level and we want to make this permanent or want to get married? What am I going to do? Just come home one day and be like, "Mom, I am engaged!" My mom started asking, "Are you and him dating?" because I would be talking about him so much. I would be like, "No, no," which would be a perfect opportunity for me to say "Yes," but I just couldn't do it. ...

Both women reflect on their allegiance to a cultural world order in the South Asian American context. Indira and Jhumpa exude the complexities of possible and simultaneous identifications within multiple contradictory sites. Here, if we can begin to imagine the women beyond a fixed sociospatial fabric of existence, then we can see that my informants' experiences signify that they are not rebelliously seeking partners.

5 Love-Cum-Arranged

The Masala-itis rebel imagery clichés about second-generation women simply fall short and fall apart. The women are not only searching for partners who will be able to follow through on Bengali traditions and participate in the women's family and community gatherings, but I also uncover my respondents do not ignore the histories and nuances within the practice of arranged marriage. The women relay that arranged marriages in the second-generation community are not uncommon, though values surrounding marriage prove to be a particularly contentious arena. My research participants map falling in love as a modern American technology and arranged marriage as traditional (read as "backward") and with South Asia. The women perceive South Asianness as patriarchal and arranged marriage as oppressive, taboo conduct, and my respondents continued to aspire to avoid identification with the Orientalist Other. Hence, the women in this study re-engineer the arranged marriage by decentering the stigmas (strict, inflexible, and patriarchal) that come along with it. I follow the trail left behind by two women in my fieldwork who participated in arranged marriages—Rita and Padmini— to further explore the diversity of actual marriage practices, which are dictated by class, religion, migratory experiences, and regional settlements of the women.

Rita agreed to have her parents support her in choosing a spouse because she wanted a partner who "click"ed with her parents and, in turn, a partner whom her parents would approve of:

> I did not want to do it [arranged marriage] because I had a bad impression of that whole process ... [But] my dad completely rationalized everything. He was, "If you haven't met anyone, then why not let us introduce you to people? Wouldn't you let your friends introduce you to people?" [And] I have always had a very strong sense of duty to my parents. I have never wanted to disappoint them, and I know that my parents would not be able to click as well [with a non-desi]....

It was paramount for Padmini to be married to someone who was familiar with Bengali Hindu culture and Padmini's parents also assisted her to select a spouse: "It was something very prominent in my mind [to marry] someone who can understand the language [my parents] speak ... I was looking for somebody who knew their food and who knew their mannerisms." Like the Kutchi Hindu Gujarati women in Ramji's (2003) ethnography in Northwest London, the reasons for wanting to be part of a tightly knit community and intricate marriage network are not necessarily intrinsic to the culture and tradition of these women but are part of their identity formation developed in the South Asian American context.

However, it is precisely within the diasporic context that also draws the women's attention to cultural practices in conjunction with an essentialized concept of culture, sanctioning South Asianness as patriarchal and arranged marriage as taboo conduct. Rita's second-generation cousins felt that she was a "sell out" because she agreed to an arranged marriage:

> [I really had to defend myself] when I agreed to do the whole arranged marriage thing. I really felt like I had to justify it to my cousins. They were like, "I don't believe you are going to give in to this." They really couldn't believe it and it almost felt like I was selling out because we've always

been kind of united against our parents, and that kind of set me apart ...
I think that once I agreed to start meeting people through my parents,
they almost were disappointed.

Like Rita's cousins, my research participants aspired to avoid identification
with the Orientalist Other, fashioning an Orientalist distinction between
"arranged marriage" and "love marriage." Nadia narrates arranged marriage as
an oppressive act imposed on women:

> A lot of the girls that I grew up with are all getting arranged. The parents
> just pick someone, and the girls say yes. They see some black ass guy from
> Bangladesh who came [here], and they just get married. You see the wed-
> ding pictures where the girl is real pretty and the guy has thick ass glasses,
> and he is nasty. I am just like, "Why?"

Tina links arranged marriage to women and domestic labor:

> The way I perceive [arranged marriage] is the way my cousins have been
> raised in India ... There is a focus on marriage and getting married right
> away after you complete your education. There is a focus on the tradi-
> tional role of a wife or mother and not really given the chance to explore
> your career.

Nadia and Tina equate arranged marriage to brown women to domestic labor
and lack of agency. Both women's Orientalist representation of South Asian
women as subservient victims ready to be consumed by the male gaze illustrates the significance of Orientalism to middle-class U.S. notions of identity
and modernity. Nadia and Tina reproduce an Orientalist logic that renders
South Asian women as "requiring [w]estern discovery, intervention, or liberation" (Naber 2006, 106). My informants imagine arranged coupling experiences as "backward" and unamerican. Rani considers herself to be "more
American than Indian" because she decided to marry a Malayalam Christian,
while her family are orthodox Hindu Brahmans. Rani articulates she chose an
exogamous partner based on her individual desire (read as American) versus
preserving collective family honor (read as South Asian):

> I believe in falling in love, being proposed to, and getting married—[the]
> traditional western ideal. I don't value some of the Bengali marriage cus-
> toms, like arranged marriages, following a caste system, and even when
> it's time for the wedding [based on horoscope matching] ... I don't value

the culture of guilt, duty, and fear of shaming the family that is put upon children in Indian culture.

Anita discerns, "the only and right way to marry is to wait for the right person rather than exchanging biodatas." She expands, "I want to get married, but I don't want to get married for the sake of getting married. I want to get married because at the end of the day, you know it's someone you want to grow old with." The taboos around arranged marriage are informed by the Third World Woman trope, that South Asian women are domesticated and lack agency (Puar 1994a, 24). Auditi refused to have a marriage arranged for her:

> I was raised with a very strong message: I belonged to [my parents] and it was for them to make decisions for me, and then it would be my husband making decisions for me ... There was always the expectation that I was going to have an arranged marriage, and when I tried to challenge my parents on that, which I did, I was a bad daughter for having done that ... I think I was just really ready to step up to my parents and say I am not going to fit into any of those definitions that you've laid out for me as a woman, what my responsibility is, or what my role is, or anything else.

Auditi uses Mohanty's construction of the monolithic Third World Woman—through color equals culture—to write off the complexities of arranged marriage.

Agency in romantic partnership—falling in love and choosing whom to marry and when to marry—is of great consequence then, especially for my desi respondents. Padmini veils her arranged marriage, offering a counter-memory to consolidate the American nation-state:

> None of my friends know the story of how I got married. I didn't even tell them when I was first engaged. I didn't want them to know after three dates with someone that my parents chose for me, I was getting married. I think [my friends] would have expected more from me. I don't think my friends knew me as someone who would take that, but lo and behold, I did. Rather than an explanation, I gave people a totally alternative story, because I didn't think that they could understand the explanation.

The persistent "east/west": tradition/modern discourse paints a "free" and "democratic" America and informs Padmini's myth as a second-generation South Asian American woman. Grewal (1994) writes, "The discourse of 'freedom' is essential to the consolidation and ongoing construction of "western" state structures ..." (59). The forgoing contested myths suggest that we tend to remember (or not remember) events that proceed according to a certain schematic set of prior expectations, resulting in historical narratives becoming "verbal fictions" (White 1978). While Padmini's arranged marriage is a secret, Rita uses "falling in love" rhetoric to describe her arranged marriage, bridging the gap between social traditions and her attitudes about dating and marriage by both breaking and supporting Orientalist discourse:

> I could tell he was nervous, which is kind of charming in a weird way. We talked for two and a half hours [on the phone] ... We talked about not very generic things. It was almost like we had known each other. It was weird. I asked my parents to tell me more about this guy because I had kind of felt something.

Rita reconfigures her arranged courtship and marriage narrative to standardize or conform to American ideals of romance and marriage. The women's interviews shed light on the relationship between South Asian women and feminism (read as "western"), a relationship that renders an activist wearing a hijab or connecting the words "Islam" and "feminism" impossible (Puar 1994a, 84–85). South Asian women as an exploited and oppressed category serve to build the "free and independent American woman" (Grewal 1994, 59). Within this comparison, South Asia is a uniformly oppressive place for women and America is the land of the free. The misguided perception of gender equality in the United States is rooted in European colonial discourse. The binary formulation ignores women's exploitation in the United States and denies women's agency in South Asia. Yet, Rita simultaneously submerges the image of universal arranged marriage. First, Rita underscores her agency in her arranged marriage:

> I told my mom that my rules are probably different than most people who agree to this process. I told her I did not want to exchange pictures because I don't want it to be based on looks. Second, I don't want them to only pick someone for me to meet based on their biodata. If I am going to give someone a chance, it is going to be everyone. This is not a job interview, and I am not going to date someone off their résumé.

Second, Rita challenges whiteness and the Orientalist cultural conquest:

> It's not like where within a couple of days you decide if you want to marry him and then there is an engagement. It's not like that. Still, in

an American's eyes, it's arranged. But what's strange about it is if it were two Americans meeting through their parents, it wouldn't be arranged. It would be a setup; it would be like a blind date!

Padmini and Rita's contradictions speaks to their ambiguous privileges of class and nation, resulting in multiply shifting and positioned subjectivities. Visweswaran (1994) suggests that contradiction (and silence) is a site of resistance to social structures (and to hegemonic ethnographic practices). Listening to contradictions is a tool for examining the unvoiced workings of cultural ideology and resistance. The emergence of contradictory and complex experiences foregrounds the multiplicities of the women's identities.

CHAPTER 9

Tropologies of Queerness

Sexuality, Family, and Culture

Much of queer theory in the U.S.[1] is based on the white male experience and privilege, excluding BIPOC folx and severely limiting its relevance to "third world" activism (Ingram et al. 1997; Islam 1998; Kawale 2003). The limitation leaves many of us who identify with LGBTQIA+ communities unable to make sense of this canon. Doubly marginalized women like the late Gloria E. Anzaldúa have been thinking and writing about their experiences at intersectional locations, but the way their experiences are framed in philosophy and social theory remain uncomfortably simplistic. Queer theory in the United States continues to be thin on thinking through its intersections with gender and race. Too often, the limitations due to undertheorized South Asian LGBTQIA+ histories, compounded with a queer canon overwrought with the "east/west": tradition/modern equation, renders queer South Asian Americans as a monolithic homogenous category with little or no agency. Within the last three decades, chronicles from desi diasporic LGBTQIA+ communities in America, like *A Lotus of Another Color* (Ratti 1993) and *Impossible Desires* (Gopinath 2005), appeared, critically challenging "western" feminism and mainstream LGBTQIA+ theory and adopting an intersectional approach (à la Mohanty). Yet, the richness and contradictions that characterize our communities continue to be stifled with Indian-centric and Hindu-centric paradigms.

South Asian American LGBTQIA+ community members find it enormously difficult to construct fluid identities within the available LGBTQIA+ canon. The failure of "western" feminism to theorize BIPOC and "global south"/"third world" folx properly and critically result in monolithic subject (or object) epistemology (Mohanty 1988). Islam (1998), in her seminal study about South Asian women who love other women, found her respondents reject identifying as lesbian. South Asian American women who sought lesbian organizations and communities—white lesbians define these spaces—felt they were marginalized and exoticized (essentialized notions of race, gender, and culture). Islam's respondents consistently described women in saris and *shalwar kameezes*

---

1   This chapter is based on Badruddoja, R. (2008). Queer spaces, places, and gender: The tropologies of Rupa and Ronica. *Feminist Formations, 20*(2), 156-88.

would never be seen as lesbians in America. The women, additionally, discussed growing up with breasts, hips, and long hair, an aesthetic value system utterly different from white androgyny. Most women expressed their bodies were reinterpreted by white lesbians as manifestations of being femme. Brah (1996) finds Asian women are codified as passive, dependent, quiet, sensitive, and gentle. And Khan (1993) uncovers South Asian American women believe white folk see them through imperialist eyes, which requires South Asians to either integrate or abandon their Asianness. The informants unanimously convey white women believe that sexism is a more fundamental problem than racism. The studies address the oppression of racism in mainstream LGBTQIA+ history. Ingram et al. (1997) explain, "Women, people of colour, and transgendered people are wrestling with the complex array of differences and similarities that complicate the building of alliances, and few canons exist to help define the specific subjectivities of women, people of colour and transgendered people" (7). South Asian movements have been excluded from LGBTQIA+ history, literature, and media in the United States. The hegemonic LGBTQIA+ culture marginalizes the desi American experiences and lumps all nonwhite women under umbrella terms like "lesbians of color" or "queers of color," denying differences and rendering us static and generic (Mohanty (1988) uses this space to offer a better theoretical model of intersectionality).

In this chapter, I address the under documentation of the lives of queer South Asian Americans and their responses to normative forms of power. I adopt the spirit of *Queers in Space* (Ingram et al. 1997) and *Queering Bollywood* to visit paradoxes, difficulties, unity, and diversity by further unraveling the lives of two of my interviewees who self-identify as queer—Rupa and Ronica. The ethnographic data shows my respondents' experiences as "South Asian American women" depart from their counterparts in the dimension of space. More plainly, the point of departure lies in access to space. Space is a signifier of a group's status in society (Brady 2002, 7–8) and for the marginalized uneven development in space has compounded their sense of isolation (Ingram et al. 1997, 6). In nodding to Rich's (1986) "politics of location," Rupa and Ronica's stories address the under lying homophobia resulting in a complex limitation of movement and self-expression. Both respondents are out there floating even more disconnected from communities, limiting their access to resources and networks than their heterosexual identified counterparts. In the pages to come, I explore Rupa's and Ronica's painful struggles to weave supportive spaces for themselves. The interviews bring to light how and why Rupa and Ronica consciously forgo community-building in white mainstream spaces. They remain resilient in maintaining ties with South Asian communities, especially with their parents and the diasporic communities in which they grew up. At the same time, Rupa and Ronica emphasize desi spaces are not alto-gether a different conception of spatiality. Like white hegemonic spaces, desi spaces homogenize race, class, sexuality, gender, and nation. As a result, Rupa and Ronica live, work, and play in "alternative 'brown'" spaces. My informants intentionally recreate their South Asian culture and the familial by deliberately inserting themselves in brown networks outside of the heterosexual matrix. In re-creating their family, Rupa and Ronica challenge South Asian and American ideologies that read blood as the key foundation to kinship (Naber 2006, 102). Meaning, Rupa and Ronica demonstrate families are contextually defined. In addition, my interviewees locate an alternative to the South Asian/queer split (Naber 2006, 98–104). Being South Asian and queer are core identity markers for Rupa and Ronica and they manipulate social ties to create safe spaces for themselves that speak to being queer without forging their culture. Rupa and Ronica build what it means to be queer and South Asian as they understand it. They arduously navigate the spaces between subjective, lived experiences and discursive, applied definitions to demonstrate South Asian American and queer identities are far more than simple and linear. In the end, Rupa and Ronica exhibit how they accept, manipulate, and resist hegemony.

1   Rupa

1.1   *Not Muslim ... but Muslim*
I begin to unravel Rupa's journey through her romantic experiences. As part of the hetero-normative and paternalistic matrix, Rupa found herself in a series of fleeting relationships with men, mostly white, while in college, and by her sophomore year, she was in an exclusive relationship with a second-generation Korean American man. Within weeks of their courtship, Rupa was caught in a web of physical violence: "We started dating and within two weeks he had raped me ... I thought because it happened that I had to be with him, and I didn't call it rape at the time." She found solace from the ongoing physical and mental abuse by forming close ties with another man who was a part of her larger social circle in college:

> At that same time, I started to become close to [another guy] ... We cooked together, smoked weed together, and opened the dictionary and read funny words to each other ... Everything with [my boyfriend] was getting worse and worse ... Then somewhere in the beginning of that winter quarter, [my friend] and I made out ... That was the thing that gave me the impetus to break up with [my boyfriend].

Fostering an intimate relationship with her friend provided Rupa with the inner strength to leave her abuser. By the end of her sophomore year, Rupa entered a committed and monogamous romantic partnership with her friend, and the trauma from her previous relationship followed her into her new one. Rupa suffered from severe bouts of depression, incapacitating her. She was unable to get out of bed in the morning and attend her lectures. Rupa dropped out of a Midwestern Ivy League school during her junior year and moved to the West Coast to live with her best friend.

Rupa desperately required time away from school, her boyfriend, and her parents to work through intimate partnership violence trauma. She turned to cigarettes, drugs, and alcohol to dissipate her pain: "After all that stuff with [my ex-boyfriend], I started smoking every day, drinking, and doing drugs ...." Rupa's parents (on the East Coast) confronted her about the drug and alcohol abuse over the phone. They strongly advised Rupa to think about her health along with what community members, especially religious leaders, would say about her and the family if they found out about her substance abuse. More importantly, Rupa's parents were concerned about what Allah would think of her. They sternly warned that her recent actions were un-Islamic, and she was risking going to hell: "[My parents said,] 'It is un-Islamic. What are people going to say? We have worked so hard for you, and now you are going to do this! We know what is best for you. Don't you know you are going to go to hell for this?'" The parental intervention ended with Rupa renouncing Islam: "I was nineteen. I was at the point where I said, 'I am not Muslim.'"

Soon after, Rupa made the difficult decision to attend her brother's high school graduation on the East Coast. Upon arriving at home, both family and community members reminded her that dropping out of school, living with a friend, and remaining idle and drinking, smoking, and doing drugs will only serve to destroy the path of success her physician parents have worked so hard to secure for her:

> With the only credit card that I had, I got a plane ticket to go home for my brother's [high school] graduation. But it was horrible ... They wanted me to stay at home. I think if I stayed at home and promised never to do these things again, they would have been happier somehow ... [They wanted me to be] the absolute ideal [daughter]: Five-times-a-day-praying, regular Koran-reading, a daughter who goes to her classes and makes good grades, goes to Muslim Student Association meetings, and ask[s] her parents' guidance in finding the right life partner for her ... It was mostly framed in religious kind of things.

Once again, religious discourse—Islam—was used to frame the second attempt at intervention. During the graduation celebrations, Rupa felt she needed to partially sever her ties with her parents and the Muslim community in her small hometown on the East Coast.

Rupa returned to her best friend's place feeling horribly inadequate as a Bengali Muslim daughter (in America). Her boyfriend supported her to reaffirm her value as a human being: "[My boyfriend] was on the phone with me every day. I was a wreck, like ready to have a nervous breakdown. At one point on the phone, he said, 'If you tell me that you need me, I'll come.' I told him that I needed him, and he came to rescue me." Rupa returned to the Midwest to live with her boyfriend while he completed his senior year in college. Despite having limited contact with her family, Rupa felt it was time her parents knew about her significant other. She again traveled home to inform them of her intimate partnership. Unsurprisingly, she used antireligious discourse to frame her relationship with her white American boyfriend:

> Over the summer, when I moved with [him], I told them. I also told them that I wasn't Muslim at that time ... I didn't know how else to explain it without telling them, "Okay, this is the person that I love." What ended up happening was that I was disowned ... "You are not our daughter, and we are not going to financially support you."

Rupa left her childhood home feeling empty and lost for a second time. Weeks later, Rupa's community priest or imam contacted her. The imam urged her to come back home yet again so that he could mediate a solution between her and her parents. Rupa, hesitant, took him up on his offer, only to be forced to leave for campus that night:

> He called me, "Betti [my daughter], I know it is not your fault. I know it is hard growing up here. Please come home. You and your parents should at least be talking face to face. I will mediate." I agreed, and my parents sent me a plane ticket. Everything turned upside down. I got home, and all my posters were taken down from the walls, and all the stuff that was me was just gone. I met with the Imam for two or three hours, and he was such an ass. He said, "This is your fault. What are you doing? This is totally unacceptable. Nobody is going to support you if you take this route." I went home that day.

Rupa describes the experiences as an emotionally wounding déjà vu.

Undoubtedly, a centrifugal theme in Rupa's herstory has been her family and religious community's decisions to label her life choices as un-Islamic. Her parents' words began to haunt her: "Don't you know you are going to hell for this?" To protect her own sense of morality, Rupa distanced herself from a Muslim identity. Yet, Rupa could not quite obliterate her link to Islam, and she thinks about the implications of being a Muslim (woman) in America, often correcting misconceptions about Muslims and defending the religion:

> I remember having this discussion about the word "Jihad" [with my boy-friend] and I said, "Jihad doesn't mean holy war. The actual word means striving or struggle." He said, "No ... it is like this really religious and war-mongering society." I said, "No, and I don't identify with that religion, but that is not all it is." It was interesting because I didn't identify as Muslim, but I knew that was part of me somehow because I really felt it was an attack on my people and me.

Rupa describes a spiritual awakening and religious epiphany during a trip to Bangladesh (one of her ancestral homelands) several years ago:

> It is rice patty fields, barley &elds, and just miles and miles of wetland ... I felt so completely at home. It was bizarre ... I felt utterly centered. I felt like the earth was rising to meet my feet. I would walk inside the house, which was red clay, and it felt like [it] was embracing me ... It came from the actual land, the actual air, the sky, and the water ... It was like a spiritual awakening. That was the moment I think I went from like, "I am not Muslim, I think I am an atheist, to the Goddess exists and she is at least partly [in me]."

When she thinks about her racial, ethnic, cultural, and religious heritage, she feels "rocktortan", or the calling of blood ties in Bengali. Rupa conjures up the following imagery: "Fragmented, Bengali, migration, partition, communal violence, refugees, and I think about food, spirit, gin, and myths. I think about ancestry and all the women on my mom's side of the family. I think *rocktortan* and the pull of land." The pull of her ancestral land cajoles Rupa to defend and uphold Bangladesh, Bangladeshis, and Islam:

> In high school, whenever we studied Islam or South Asia in social studies, I was always defending it. They always portrayed Bangladesh as this poor, ravaged, starving, awful, terrible place. I would do what I could and talk about its [beauty]. My social studies teacher in ninth grade was an idiot.

He said that Bangladesh was named after the Bengal tiger and I said, "no." Whenever we studied religion, the only images I saw of Muslims in our textbooks were men in turbans with machine guns, so I was defending that as well ... I had a lot of pride in where I came from, even though all I wanted to do was fit in.

Rupa, in her thirties, confidently identifies as a Muslim woman:

I have an extremely small community of Muslims that I identify with, my spiritual community. They are mostly like me. Yes, I think Islam in essence is this beautiful religion, and I think that it has been totally warped by patriarchy. I believe that Islam is about peace, justice, love, and divine love.

Rupa's personal identification as a Muslim is linked to her Bangladeshi heritage, underscoring religious choices often stem from racial and ethnic projects (Bashi 1998).

Another watershed in Rupa's life is when her *nani*, or maternal grandmother, suffered from a debilitating stroke in Bangladesh. It proved to be the beginning of the repair process between Rupa and her parents:

My grandmother had a stroke in Bangladesh ... That killed me. I told my dad on the phone, "Look, if amma is going back, and I don't know if she wants this or not, but if she wants me to come, I will go with her." I talked to my mom a few days later, and she told me that she wanted me to go with her. I think that was the turning point for them. They thought that whatever terrible decisions she is making, she still loves us, and that did it.

After Rupa's trip to Bangladesh to visit her grandmother, Rupa rejuvenated her ties with her mother and father and returned to school part time: "I was going [to school] part time now. After the whole thing with my nani, my parents told me that they loved me and they didn't approve of anything that I was doing, but they would send me back to school if I wanted." Rupa was relieved that her parents were beginning to accept some of the decisions she had made about her life and refrained from demoralizing her through religion.

1.2   *Challenging Whiteness, Patriarchy, and Heteronormativity*

Rupa's boyfriend graduated and unexpectedly moved to the West Coast for a job opportunity. The distance took a toll on their relationship. Rupa and her boyfriend drifted apart, and he cheated on her: "[My boyfriend] moved back to the [West Coast], and he cheated on me with a teenager [there] ... We should never have tried the long-distance thing. We had really grown apart at that point, but I had left my family for him, so I couldn't even imagine anything else." The break-up with her boyfriend was yet another fault line in her life:

> In the end it was good. I think it was sometime when I was with him [that I realized that I was queer] ... If he weren't around to rescue me with our relationship, I think I would have started dating women much sooner. Even when we were dating, I felt like it didn't matter what sex or gender a person is, and I wasn't transgender aware at that time. But it didn't matter if it was a guy or girl; it mattered who the person was. I always carried that with me.

Rupa recognized that she was queer. Parting ways with her boyfriend also helped her to develop some rules about whom she will not date. Like many of the women in the study, one of Rupa's critical rules involves a bar on white men: "Currently, I am attracted to men, like bio men, but I am just going to say it is no to white boys ... The whole thing of the white man [is that] there is such privilege there, and it has just gone unrecognized or unacknowledged that there is that privilege difference." Rupa struggles with her "no white boys" rule because she is once again in an intimate relationship with a white man. She circumvents her struggles by cogently emphasizing that he was not born with white male privilege: "It just gets complicated [when I say] I am not going to date any white boys. He is white, and he identifies as a boy, but there is a difference because he wasn't born with the same privilege." Rupa's boyfriend identifies as a transgender man.

1.3   Subjectivity and Managing Identities (Sexuality, Family, and Culture)

Rupa encounters several watersheds, which grant her back-and- forth movement, like a pendulum, between her individual conscious and collective conscious. The reflexive relationship between the "I" and "Me" (à la Mead) incites a fear of losing her parents. This has always been a central concern for Rupa, especially when she makes choices different from theirs: "From the time I was nineteen, I have lived my life as I needed to, [but] I think, whenever [I] made those decisions, my first reaction was always fear about what was going to happen, and fear of losing my family in the past, and I still do." Rupa, therefore, has not shared her queer identity with most of her family members. She says, "I am out to my younger brother; he is the only person in the family that knows that." Rupa was disowned once for abusing drugs and alcohol and for dating a white man. She did not want to begin to think about how her parents would react and what they would do to her if they found out she is queer. Through silence, both Rupa and her parents are mutually implicated in keeping the idealized notions of South Asianness and Americanness active in opposition. The silence keeps the binary intact and effaces that the heterosexual imperative maintains the points of opposition as one and the same (Naber 2006, 97–98).

Rupa's experiences plainly suggest that since the age of nineteen, she has made life decisions that she thought were best for her at the time. She led her life as she needed to, often ostracized by the familial and community collective she was raised in. Her sophomore year in college proved to be a pivotal time in Rupa's life: an amalgam of potent events that took place—an abusive intimate relationship, incapacitating depression, disowned by her family, renouncing her religion, and a codependent intimate relationship—helped her to probe her sexuality. Rupa was successful in uncovering her sexual identity, but she found that her sexual calling was at odds with her racial, ethnic, cultural, and religious background. Kawale is helpful here: "Being under considerable surveillance from South Asian communities, the managing of multiple identities such as ethnicity and sexuality is an essential part of South Asian women's subjectivity, whether they are heterosexual, lesbian or bisexual" (193–94). The conceptualization of identity helps us to appreciate Rupa's inability to combine her religious identity as a Muslim with her sexuality.

But surprisingly, Rupa triumphantly talks about her boyfriend in conversations with her parents. She simply disguises him as her female roommate and best friend. "[My parents] don't know that Sam is *he*, but they hear 'Samantha.' The have never met him. They don't know what it is. The hear best friends. I talk about Samantha all the time." Since their time together, Rupa and her boyfriend have had numerous conversations about taking their relationship to another level of commitment. Because their relationship falls far outside the heterosexual matrix, Rupa is unsure what that partnership would look like, what it would mean, and how she might integrate him into her family life. Rupa voices,

> I know that it would not be worth it for me to have [my boyfriend] and lose my whole family for it … [My boyfriend] and I would throw out these insane ideas about how we would work around this. There is the crazy idea of [my boyfriend] transitioning and converting to Islam, and they will never know. I mean physical transition. It was a joke before, but

it is not a joke anymore, and it's not even funny anymore. [Maybe] I'll find a gay boy to marry who is [South Asian] and Muslim and be in the same boat.

Rupa ponders if it is even worth carrying on a relationship with someone her parents would never approve of. The following excerpt is yet another lucid example speaking to Rupa's performance of her sexuality, family, and culture over a single spatial-temporal context. Rupa is an actor, artist, and poet working for an all-women, Asian-American and Pacific Islander collective involved in multimedia and multidisciplinary theater and performance art. Rupa describes one of her recent shows, a show in which her father came to see her perform on stage for the first time:

> For this show, I don't think we have said "pussy" more times in a single set. I was freaking out. I had myself taken out of one of the pieces called "Fiercely Fem" so it wouldn't be me directly saying these things. Even so, I was seriously stressed that they were going to start to wonder ... The night before, I had barely slept ... That whole day I was physically ill with fear. Before every show, we circle up and dedicate the performance to someone in our lives. I said that my family is going to be here tonight; the show is for them....

Rupa was relieved her parents were able to attend the show but had missed the sets that may point to her sexuality. Rupa wonderfully demonstrates instances of how she begins to think about managing her queer identity while also preserving her relationship with her parents and culture.

Rupa, without a doubt, innovatively lives her life as she needs to while maintaining resilient ties with her family. She also productively rebuilds an alternative familial and cultural community through her all-women-of-color performing arts collective. Rupa actively constructs spaces and places that foster diversity without policing, surveillance, and erasure, where the familial is reconstructed outside the heterosexual matrix (Butler 1997). She demonstrates that she has uncovered ways in which to realize her religion and ethnicity performatively and sexuality together, through redefinition rather than forgoing one for the other. Like the British South Asian lesbian women in Kawale's (2003) study, Rupa generates new ways of doing gender, ethnicity, and sexuality to identify as a gender-queer South Asian American Muslim woman. Rupa certainly offers possibilities of re-homing.

2   Ronica

2.1   Rupturing White/Feminist/Queer Canon

Ronica begins to develop her narrative through key words, phrases, and labels she often uses to identify herself with and what being the labels means to her. First, Ronica, while comfortable with the pronoun "she", refuses to categorize herself as male or female. She self-identifies as gender-queer:

> There is this strong gender binary of what is feminine and what is mas-culine. [But] gender is a continuum just as much as sexuality is to me. It has been more recent for me to think about myself as being this gender-queer person, and although I identify as a female, I don't really feel like, "Oh, I am this 100% woman...." Yeah, [I still mark "female" on a form], but I think that that's probably wrong these days, especially seeing my friends' [gender] transitions.

Second, Ronica identifies as a South Asian, a Bengali from Calcutta:

> I feel South Asian is a political identity and I believe in that identity. I would say I was South Asian and then Bengali. I would probably say I was from India and Calcutta. I end up bonding with South Asians who are queer in a way that I can't really bond with anybody else.

Ronica indicates being gender-queer and South Asian American is an elabo-rate identity that combines gender, sexuality, race, ethnicity, and cultural con-structions into a cohesive category.

The intersections among these specific categories often leave Ronica feeling alienated from the larger queer community in America. As a queer Bengali American, Ronica was initially afraid of judgment from broader queer move-ments about her Hindu Bengali cultural practices. She provides an example of selectively wearing desi clothing: "I could probably wear a *shalwar* or a sari to hang out with my friend, [but] I would wear them in places where I wouldn't feel totally uncomfortable." Ronica enjoys wearing desi clothing to increase her visibility and affirm her South Asianness, but only with certain people in par-ticular venues. Ronica's queer South Asian friends provide her with a space in which she can exert control over being seen through dress and assert positively a combination of her sexuality and ethnicity. But she is unlikely to wear saris or *shalwars* to "white venues," where she dresses in "appropriate" clothing (invis-ibility/assimilation). Ronica is concerned with queer South Asians in America not having a safe place to articulate their cultures: "I'm afraid of queer [South

Asians] never having a place to integrate [South Asian] culture." Part of the predicament is that her coming-out process was framed within the confines of a Eurocentric sexual agenda:

> When I first came out as being queer, I felt I was excluded from the queer community because I didn't really know Asian people, South Asian people, or people of color that were queer … The dominant discourse in the queer community is based around white people, and that's really alienating.

Kawale (2003) writes about the struggles for cultural authenticity within the South Asian lesbian community in Britain. While Ronica vehemently rejects a lesbian identity, Kawale's study is nevertheless applicable:

> White women in lesbian spaces are more likely to be considered as lesbians tha[n] are South Asian women. For example … one of my interviewees [with a group of friends] … [were] asked [by] the white (male) bouncer … whether they were aware it was gay night … and whether they were indeed lesbians. [My interviewee] interpreted this and other similar experiences with white women as a racism driven by the assumption that 'South Asian women can't be lesbians', especially if they have long hair. (185)

Ronica and Kawale problematize the powerful role of the white gaze in queer activism and theory. Both Ronica and Kawale's discussion around the insignificance of race and ethnicity in the realms of gender and sexuality illuminate that the American and "western" conception of queer needs to be reconceptualized along transnational terms for diasporic queers like Ronica. Ingram et al. (1997) follow: "The majority of people who 'run' visibly queer ghettos and municipalities are white, middle-class gay men" (7). Mirza (1997) explains:

> [Whiteness is a] powerful places that makes invisible, or re-appropriates things, people, and places it does not want to see or hear, and the[n] through misnaming, renaming or not naming at all, invents truth—what we are told is "normal," neutral, universal, simply becomes the way it is. (3)

Fanon (1986) states, "[n]ot only must the black man be black; he must be black in relation to the white man" (110). Ronica finds, then, that racism and imperialism are not necessarily consequential issues shared by white LGBTQIA+

members. Race and racialized markers are a fundamental schism between Ronica and the larger queer community, and the white/feminist/queer community does not adequately meet her needs of collectivity.

Unable to accept the mainstream American construction of queer identity, Ronica, who traverses a complex web of social and political structures, involves herself in a small queer South Asian and of color network. Ronica feels more dedicated to the South Asian community and being with other desi LGBTQIA+ people is valuable to her: "When I hang out with a bunch of people of color who are queer, including South Asian people and whatever, doing it feels really good to me. I feel more dedicated to [South Asians] now." Ronica's insistence in breaking down the opposition between white/feminist/queer culture and South Asian culture is an act of resisting racism on multiple fronts: It undermines the South Asian/queer binary that seek to control women's sexuality by marking women who transgress the heterosexual imperative of an imagined South Asian cultural authenticity as "American," and it disrupts the dualistic logic of hegemonic U.S. nationalist discourse that homogenize and subordinate South Asian women as victims of male and family control or exotic erotic objects accessible to white/western male "heroes" (Naber 2006, 102–103).

With nostalgia, Ronica explains venues that are apart from mainstream queer networks provide her with an extended family atmosphere:

> The place I feel most comfortable in the world—and that doesn't happen that much—[is] when there is a bunch of people in the room who don't speak each other's language very well, but they are committed to communicating with each other ... It feels comfortable because communication isn't based on your language skills or your ability to navigate smoothly within a culture. Rather, it is based upon your appreciation of each other and the fact that you want to share this moment together.

Music is yet another space in which Ronica finds comfort:

> [I'm in a] marching band ... The idea is that we bring musical ideas into the street that hopefully will influence activist culture to be less myopic and to not have this sense of some lanky white guy with a guitar is what defines activism in America or culture ... My band does [this one] song Ranga Barsey [a song from one of Amitabh Bhachan's Hindi-language movies]. It is me singing and then a bunch of white and American people doing the call-in response. I love this idea that I am teaching them something and they are responding to it. I think there needs to be a concept of trans-culturalization in our culture, in our creating culture, and our

creating subculture and counterculture, because otherwise it becomes cultural imperialism. ...

Rich's politics of location is fruitful. Since the mid-1980s, several exciting events have heralded the emergence of Asian LGBTQIA+ movements in the United States. The formation of *Alliance of Massachusetts Asian Lesbians and Gay Men* (AMALGM); *Trikone*, a Bay area gay and lesbian newsletter; and *Shamakami*, a forum for South Asian feminist lesbians and bisexual women, has added new and welcome voices to the LGBTQIA+ communities in America (S. Islam 1993). Within the last three decades, San Francisco and New York City have become spatial sites that are South Asian- and LGBTQIA+-friendly. Ronica's insertion in LGBTQIA+ communities outside of the white/feminist/queer construct demonstrates her movement from the margin to the center. Meeting in spaces that allow her to positively express both her queerness and South Asianness enables her to define space from the position of the subject rather than the object (Kawale 2003, 186). In the end, Ronica reconfigures and transgresses both queer white feminist imperatives and imagined "true" South Asian culture.

2.2   Negotiating the Model Minority Myth

My perception of Ronica is that she is an imaginative person with immense healing powers and the resiliency to withstand arduous struggles. Whenever time and money permit, Ronica offers free services as an acupuncturist, combined with her training in homeopathic medicine, to comfort and heal sex workers in Calcutta's red-light district. The aura of self-confidence and empathy for others embraces and exudes from her. Yet, Ronica describes how her parents and the community she grew up in on the East Coast do little to accept her. Ronica's life choices are not aligned with the prescriptions put forth by middle-class white American society and the model South Asian American community: "To me, the typical South Asian [aesthetic] is about the typical [Midwestern] white [aesthetic]. I don't get the Midwestern white values that my parents would like me to have, and a lot of their friends' kids have. They are embarrassed." Ronica recounts accompanying her parents to an Indian grocery store in Edison, New Jersey, with her brightly colored hair and multiple body piercings and tattoos: "When I go out with my family, my parents are always embarrassed of me because there is a lot of pointing that happens ... That is more about otherness than anything else. I don't know what kind of otherness to define that as." Traveling with her parents to a local park is not any easier: "I think they are equally embarrassed of me in both those settings." To ease the embarrassment, Ronica attempts to "tone down" her appearance when she

is with her parents, especially during pujas or other Hindu prayers and festivals: "I always go with my friends, so I am lost in the crowd ... [but] I always
tone down the way I look." Expectedly, Ronica chooses not to bring her friends
to her parents' home, and in turn, she is unable to integrate her family life with
her friends. She describes it as dysphoria:

> I think they [family and friends] are a big source of conflict for me. The
> other day I went home to hang out with family, and it felt really alienat-
> ing after a while. Even though there are ways I relate to my family that
> I can't relate to anybody else, my sexuality and what I think about in the
> world is not welcome in my family. I start to feel very shut down and sort
> of defensive. Then I came back, and I was hanging out with a couple of
> my friends that are white and transgendered, and it felt very alienating to
> me to hang out in this group of people who can't relate at all to my family
> reality either. There is this dysphoria feeling for me that happens.

Ronica feels explosive pressure to categorize her life in binary terms—life
with her family and life outside of her family or with her friends. Ronica's
story points to the heterocentric domestic house (Désert 1997, 22). The home's
configuration presupposes gender roles and social order of age, sexuality, and
ownership, prescribed by the spatial configuration of the home. It presupposes
who should remain in the home and who should easily traverse the boundary. Like Chicana lesbians, queer South Asian women are a threat to the South
Asian community (and the dominant white community) because their existence disrupts the established male order, and it raises the consciousness of
many South Asian women regarding their own independence and control.

    The centrifugal force in shaping Ronica's identity is being desi and queer in
conjunction. Ronica, like Rupa through her all-Asian and all-women performing arts collective, reconstructs the familial with a small group of queer South
Asian friends, "I have created a South Asian community for myself. I can talk
about what's going on with me here more than I can talk about me to my parents. Having South Asian queer friends has been so good for me," and through
community building as a teacher:

> I am a teacher; I teach martial arts. The martial arts teaching that I do is
> political. A lot of my life is spent doing political work, being an activist,
> and doing queer organizing. And it is based in multiracial environments.
> I define myself as an activist who works with people of color as much
> as possible ... It is a big part to be able to combine all these cultural and
> sexual identity places together and create curriculum.

Shah's (1998) study on South Asian lesbians in the United States is useful in establishing the links among Ronica's sexuality, gender, cultural identity, and community. Shah finds exposure to feminism, activism, and community work and defining one's sexuality often go hand in hand, especially for women.

Ronica's family is an integral component of her identity and sense of self. She remains unwilling to erase her ties with her parents and her family's strong-knit Hindu Bengali community. Islam (1998) explains, "Identity based on sexuality also has to be analyzed in terms of the complex web of social relations and the context which frames them" (76). As a result, both Ronica and her parents engage in an interesting production of the open secret act:

> They don't [know] and they don't need to. I think it would be such a huge deal. We would never recover from it ... They know it is a big part of my life to be involved with people who are queer. That is the big thing. They choose not to know ... It is an interesting combination in that my mom will sometimes ask me, but she doesn't really want to know the answer. Neither of them really wants to know that I am queer. They would rather that I just kept it to myself.

Like Rupa and her parents, through silence, Ronica and her parents mutually implicate themselves in keeping the binary between idealized notions of South Asianness and Americanness intact, while masking the opposition threaten to be one and the same. With silence and the heterosexual imperative, Ronica and Rupa demonstrate three important findings: First, through family, women and their sexuality are under surveillance and contained. Second, albeit women are no longer in the locus of their families, they experience an extended sense of self and are unwilling to sever familial ties. Third, traveling between and among spaces, the contexts shift, and, thus, the meanings of women's behavior change.

2.3   *Confronting Sexual and Ethnoracial Binaries*
Traveling between and among shifting and contradictory contexts mean Ronica continually reconstructs herself. One of her largest self-examinations, without a doubt, has been to probe her sexuality. Since the age of raging hormones, fifteen, Ronica felt romantic and sexual attraction to both men and women but was unaware that she could be attracted to the latter:

> I had always been attracted to men. In fact, I had always been attracted to women, but nobody had ever told me it was okay to be attracted to

women. I started going to clubs and realized a lot of the people I was going to clubs with were gay and I was like, "Whoa, I could do that too."

Ronica finds being queer allows her more options in dating. She is not confined by dominant gender and sexuality divides, along with other forms of stringent categorizations like race. Dating for her is a function of whom she is attracted to:

> I don't like the word lesbian. I don't like the word bisexual. I don't like the word gay very much. None of those words really fit. I feel like it has nothing to do with whom I sleep with. I think it has more to do with the idea that my sexuality isn't defined by these boxes that we get into.

Unlike popular belief, being queer does not mean Ronica is constantly in a relationship and is perpetually having sex. She emphatically says, "It is definitely not about sleeping with somebody! I haven't slept with everybody I have dated!!!" Like many women, she has thought-provoking rules about dating:

> I tend to not have monogamous relationships with people ... I tend to date men very infrequently. Honesty is a big thing for me and being open and clear about where you are coming from ... My bar is being able to really relate to somebody and enjoy their company and feel like they're an exceptional person.

What Ronica's words begin to suggest is being queer is more than a gender and sexual orientation. Here, Ronica emphasizes that "queer" is a political identity and a feeling:

> Queer to me is also a political identity but it is also a product of feeling. The word "queer" is a unifying word which encompasses so many different people, and I feel an affinity with. It's sort of how I feel about the word "South Asian." I would rather use a word for myself that includes a lot of other people, because there is strength in that, rather than to use a word that puts me in a very small category of people.

And she quickly jettisons the homosexual/heterosexual duality, a major ontological dichotomy in the United States. Foucault (1990) calls for the abolition of homosexuality and heterosexuality in favor of infinity of sexualities. Similarly, Désert (1997) explains, "'Queer' can be defined elastically to include sensibilities other than the normative with a propensity towards, but not exclusive of, the homoerotic. 'Queer' is therefore a liberating rubric encompassing multiple sensibilities exclusively or in tandem" (19). Finally, Butler (1999) argues that queerness is beyond gender—it is an attitude that begins in a place not concerned with binary oppositions. Ronica is adamant in marking the homo/hetero divide as incorrect, and she has set out to redefine it.

Just as Ronica breaks up the homosexual/heterosexual binary, she defies the dating/arranged marriage construct, complicating the how she meets people and highlighting the many nuances involved in partnership approaches. She is open to meeting potential romantic partners in a variety of ways, ranging from dance clubs to placing matrimonial advertisements in *India Abroad*:

> I don't have a specific [way of meeting people]. I told my mom after a lot of coercion that I would meet someone in an arranged setting ... The main reason I fight against it is because my parents won't put an ad that is reflective of me. If they were to put down what is true, then I would be more into it. I don't want to meet some guy who is going to be like "Who the fuck is this?"

While Ronica is not yet thinking about marriage, she is cognizant, like Rupa, her partner will never be fully integrated into her family, even if she is involved with a South Asian cisgender man:

> I think that if I was to fall in love with somebody who wasn't trans or a woman, they would have to know where I was coming from. Everyone I have dated has known, and even the men that I have dated, some of whom are South Asian, that they probably won't meet my parents. They are probably not ever going to get integrated into my family.

The significance of the current discussion is multidimensional. Queerness has not even made its way into the thinkable—"that grid of cultural intelligibility that regulates the real and the nameable" (Butler 1991, 20). Like gender and sexuality models, the identities of South Asian American women are fixated on binaries: the modern and independent South Asian women (Americanized) and the traditional and passive women. Ronica cannot even begin to locate herself within the dichotomy. Her acceptance of meeting prospective marriage partners in arranged settings shows that she embraces her South Asianness, and in parallel, she takes control of her sexuality and makes decisions to support her lifestyle, e.g., her insistence the matrimonial ads must reflect her true self.

Defying and traversing dichotomous modes of conceptions has been no facile task. Like Rupa, playing multiple and contentious roles leaves Ronica feeling that defining and performing her sense of self in non-imperialist ways is far more complex than she wants it to be:

> Figuring out how to navigate that fluidity is a lifelong process. Sometimes you are this identity and sometimes you are this identity. I get to choose that, and nobody gets to choose that for me. [But] I don't think that anyone really gets taught that you are allowed to define yourself. And so, allowing myself the freedom to define myself the way that I want is sometimes actually harder than I want it to be.

Cultural identity, for Ronica, is more than separate pieces merely coming together. It is a site of tension, pain, and alienation that is constantly in motion (Naber 2006, 103). Ronica keenly recognizes the process of categorization is far more than simple for her. While at times Ronica narrates herself as a split subject, she also understands her "worlds" are not discrete. Ronica confidently articulates her sense of self through doing work that she loves, creating art and music, and socializing with like-minded people: "I feel like my identity is pretty strong. I feel comfortable with who I am and where I am going in the world. I feel they aren't necessarily these terms that make me feel comfortable so much as the reality that I have created for myself."

Space and place are crucial to a sense of identity because "identity is not just about *who* you are but *where* you are" (Kawale 2003, 195). Ronica and Rupa demonstrate they do not lack power to construct space.

CHAPTER 10

Consolidation of the American Nation-State

South Asian Diasporic Fiction

In this near final chapter,[1] I review four popular, award-winning literary fictions: Samina Ali's *Madras on Rainy Days* (2004), Chitra Banerjee Divakaruni's *Arranged Marriage* (1995), Tanuja Desai Hidier's *Born Confused* (2002), and Jhumpa Lahiri's *The Namesake* (2003). I use these novels as sites of possible ruptures in lived experiences of second-generation Bengali American women. As a second-generation Bangladeshi Muslim American woman, I am certainly sympathetic to the South Asian diasporic novels as theories of real ruptures in our lived experiences. However, as I sociologically probe the dispersion of cultural experiences through the literary fictional narratives and compare them across situations within a set of lives in my own ethnographic work, the identity formations portrayed in popular fictions seem untenable. Too often, popular literary fictions spawned by South Asian diasporic authors for consumption by both the diaspora and "western" mainstream are laden with Orientalist dualities. The "authentic" South Asian American experience simply represents South Asia within tropes of "western" hegemonic structures, where "South Asian" and "American" are essentialized identities, never broken down into further specificity (Grewal 1993). I briefly return to the words of Rupa (see Chapter 9):

> I remember having this discussion about the word "Jihad" [with my boyfriend] and I said, "Jihad doesn't mean holy war. The actual word means struggle." He said, "No ... it is like this really war-mongering society." I said, "No, that is not all it is." It was interesting because I didn't identify as Muslim [at the time], but I knew that was part of me somehow because I really felt it was an attack on my people and me.

Insightfully, Rupa, problematizes the monolithic and linear notions of "home" and identity, both of which are often linked to a singular spatial category. Rupa begins to show us—unlike the linear teleology followed by the characters of Ali,

---

1 This chapter is based on Badruddoja, R. (2014). Third world woman, family, and marriage: South Asian diasporic fiction as a site for consolidation of the American nation-state. *South Asian Review*, 35(2), 81-104.

Divakaruni, Hidier, and Lahiri—that the nature of "second-generation" identities points to an "oscillation between post-colonial and racialized American subjectivities" (Visweswaran 1993, 309). What is being written into the diasporic narratives is a story of cultural displacement, which evades the specificity of gender and depends on stereotypical propositions about America and South Asia (Mani 1993, 34). Indeed, the cultural displacement model plays a key role in perpetuating the cultural authority of the "west" (Brady 2002).

1   Samina Ali's *Madras on Rainy Days*

To journey into the lives of South Asian American wo/men, I historically and theoretically situate our experiences by sharing a dominant framework that serves to pathologize our identities and experiences in the U.S. racial and ethnic imaginary, which is fraught with gender and class: (American) Orientalism. As part of the Orientalist phantasmatic, I cite from Ali's (2004) *Madras on Rainy Days*, a work praised by the *San Francisco Chronicle*, to examine how South Asian American identity formations are fraught with American Orientalism. Layla, the second-generation protagonist, reveals:

> I had faced this all my life, the way each country [United States and India] held a moral stance of the other. It was as though each nation had its own uniform and I wore the shirt of one, the trousers of the other, and both sides were shooting at me. ... They exchanged hamburgers for chicken curry, combined Ayurvedic and modern medicine, and swapped yoga for aerobic. I had never witnessed such confused and beguiled lovers. (26–27)

The second-generation, then, are thought to occupy a liminal zone, one between Ali's "hamburgers for chicken curry." The second-generation represent this "unbridgeable cultural divide" between the falsely constructed imperialistic notions of the "east" versus the "west." They are a conundrum or "American-Born-Confused-Desis" (ABCDs)! However, the literature (Prashad, 2000; Maira, 2002; Purkayastha, 2005) demonstrates that South Asian American wo/men are neither atomized individuals nor are they structural dopes. That is, they do their identity-work in multiple, cross-cutting, simultaneous, and contentious categories of race, ethnicity, class, gender, sexuality, and culture! We must, then, consider a couple of issues: What are the questions that need to be asked to critique Layla's words? What are some of the sites of contention within the quote? First, it is imperative to consider what the division between

America and South Asia implies here. The second question I ask—perhaps one even more imperative than the first—is, how does the division between South Asia and America affect the identity formations and performances of South Asian-Americans?

The central problem lies with Layla's "torn between two cultures" rhetoric. From "confused and beguiled lovers," the reader finds Ali's protagonist Layla caught between parental desire for conformity with cultural norms that are at odds with her American (white) peers' and her own uneasy integration (assimilation into whiteness is the benchmark) into U.S. society. Layla finds herself struggling to know her place and her identity as an ABCD. Ali, then, frames Layla's journey from America to India (for a forced marriage, which Ali falsely conflates with arranged marriage) back to America (once the marriage fails) within the "east/west": tradition/modern discourse. Mani (1993) argues that the two-culture rhetoric has a long and complex history for third-world women, and its consequences bear thinking through:

> Questions of tradition and modernity have, since the nineteenth century, been debated on the literal and figurative bodies of women. It comes as no surprise that the burden of negotiating the new world is borne disproportionately to women, whose behavior and desires, real or imagined, become the litmus test for the South Asian community's anxieties or sense of well-being. (34–45)

It should come as no surprise that the conflicting framing of Layla's identity lies in the tired narrative of choosing between family obligations and falling in love. It is here—between the nexus of family and love—that we discover that Ali attributes Layla's self-questioning to her Americanness and her sense of duty and family responsibility to her Indianness. Ali underscores this tension by juxtaposing Layla with her pregnant cousin Henna, who was gang-raped during a citywide hartal—government shutdown—in Hyderabad, meeting an untimely death, while Layla escapes from her marriage and returns to the land of the free (and individuality) with her American passport, ready to begin life once again—a normal life: "The wind rose, lifting my veil like ravens' wings. Layla. Darkness. So I was. My body hidden and safe under the chador [a long shawl], belonging only to me" (307). The implication here is that this lens establishes the view that South Asian American women are part of a strict, inflexible, patriarchal, extended South Asian family, and the "westernized" second-generation offspring have no choice but to rebel against their own culture—the classic *Masala-itis* rebel imagery (Puar 1994b). Layla portrays the anomalous "Third-World Woman" (Mohanty 1988; Grewal 1993, 233). The broader context in which Layla unhappiness is embedded contains the family as the center of conflict between South Asia and America—South Asia imagined as the ultimate site of failure, and America conceived as the sole answer to all her problems (Grewal 1993, 235).The opinions of Grewal (1993), who considers living in South Asia and being South Asian means inhabiting a "combat zone, a zone of warfare" (235); and of Mani (1993) who holds that "Americanness ... is simply an unambivalent index of cultural difference, even superiority" (36) both seem to be apt here. Clearly, Ali uses a Euro-American epistemology to formulate the subject of feminism. Minh-ha (1989) calls this portrayal one of "specialness" rather than one of difference, suggesting a division between "I-who-have-made-it and You-who cannot-make-it" (86–87). Ali's work demonstrates a rigid socio-cognitive framework from which its world is unable either to escape or to break away from compartmentalizing bodies, or reading bodies in multiple ways (Zerubavel 1991, 121).

The empirical reality is that while American Orientalism can begin to help us understand gendered and sexualized discourses of assimilation and racism faced by South Asian Americans, Orientalism is simply not enough to explain the complexities of our lives. Revisiting the words of two of my informants—Padmini and Rita—in the context of romantic relationships and marriage are helpful here (see Chapter 8). Padmini describes why it was important for her to have her parents' involvement in her selection of a partner: "It was something ... prominent in my mind [to marry] someone who can understand the language [my parents] speak ... I was looking for somebody who knew their food and who knew their mannerisms." And Rita fascinates me by submerging the image of universal arranged marriage, challenging the Orientalist cultural conquest:

> It's not like where within a couple of days you decide if you want to marry him and then there is an engagement. It's not like that. Still, in an American's eyes [read as "white"], it's arranged. But what's strange about it is if it were two Americans meeting through their parents, it wouldn't be arranged. It would be a setup; it would be like a blind date!

As a gentle reminder, the reasons for wanting to be part of a tightly knit community and of intricate marriage network are not necessarily intrinsic to the culture and tradition of these women; rather, they are part of their identity formation developed in the South Asian American context (Ramji 2003). Ali's Layla, on the other hand, portrays the anomalous "Third-World Woman" à la Mohanty (1988), and Ali falsely conflates forced marriage with arranged marriage. Simply put, Ali succeeds in binding South Asian women into a monolithic stereotype: Permissive women who are forced to forgo their individual desires, or who must leave their families behind if they choose to realize their dreams. Indeed, the practice of arranged marriage is highly problematic, raising questions of choice, economic production, reproduction, and the role of women in the society at large. However, collectively, the women's voices and stories about dating and marriage in my study complicate the picture of arranged marriage process, revealing many nuances operative in actual practice.

It is interesting to inquire why "westernization" is the expression of choice leveled against the "third world" and used to bolster the ABCD identity formation. Narayan (1997) explains that the answer lies in colonial history. Contrasting self-definitions of "western culture" and the "indigenous national culture" of colonies were constructed via political conflicts between colonialism and national movements (14–21). Within gendered, colonial, and nation-state contexts, South Asian women are subscribed to a dichotomy between the "material west" and the "spiritual east," and, like Layla, they are expected to embrace their role as "repositories of a national spiritual essence" (19). The danger here is that the language used to produce literature extends experiences in time and space. Brady (2002) writes:

> Literature thrives on the intersection between shaping powers of language and the productive powers of space. Literature attends to affect an environment; it uses space and spatial processes metaphorically to suggest emotions, insights, concepts, characters. It also shapes the way spaces are perceived, understood, and ultimately produced. Thus, literature illustrates and enlarges the shaping force of narrative in the production of space, highlighting the discursiveness of space, its dependence on cultural mediation. (8)

As a result, Layla's body becomes a "transcolonial zone" for the reader. Layla reproduces a circulation of narratives across the Atlantic, from "east" (production—the storyteller) to "west" (consumer—the reader), while Layla becomes the site of exchange between South Asia and the United States, serving as the location of "transcolonial transmission." Here I ask: Why does the material/spiritual dichotomy pose a challenge to the identities of South-Asian Americans? The binary lens leads to the naturalization of South Asian traditions, American freedom, and the uncritical acceptance of generalized assumptions. The South Asia versus America metanarrative not only prompts a reductive tabloid interpretation, but also prohibits readers from engaging in alternate readings that might highlight the wealth and complexity of the material. A passage from Zainab Ali's (1993) essay, entitled "Becoming Agents of Our Identity" may shed some light here:

> This is the first of many incidents in which I have felt like I am sitting on the border of two culture[s] and religions. This position invariably forces me into feelings of disjunction because I must choose between two cultural practices. Nevertheless, it would be wrong to assume that I am able to choose to which side of the fence I want to jump: I have no choice. Rather, I am disjointed from both my Islamic culture and my Urdu language, and my—yes, it is mine also—Western culture and English language. Which do I use to express myself? Which becomes my identity? (238)

A reductive reading of Zainab Ali's words positions her as confused, torn, and soul-searching for her identity. A less monolithic assessment, on the other hand, allows the recognition that the contours of her struggles are fundamentally shaped by her class position and gender.

To Samina Ali's credit, she develops a complex representation of women's agency within the constructs of gender, class, and sexuality. Even though there are many different stories of arrival and survival in the accounts of South Asian women, especially due to the idioms of class privilege among post-1965 immigrants from South Asia (Visweswaran 1993). "There is no rupture," says Mani (1993), "in patriarchal power with migration, merely its reconfiguration, the consequences of diaspora are specifiably different for men and women" (33–34). This means that class benefits are tempered by femaleness. Layla finds ways to host a white, male lover who had no problems sneaking into her bedroom because she did not have the courage to sneak out of her parents' home in the middle of the night. Samina Ali also vividly illustrates Layla's efforts in terminating her pregnancy from that relationship soon after she arrives in India for her marriage. The sexual experimentation between Layla and her female cousin Henna also shows the ways in which Layla manipulates the dynamics of gender and culture in multiple ways.

It may be useful to explore two other popular fictions: Chitra Banerjee Divakaruni's *Arranged Marriage* (1995), and Tanuja Desai Hidier's *Born Confused* (2002).

2   **Chitra Banerjee Divakaruni's** *Arranged Marriage*

The voices of immigrant South Asian American women in Chitra Banerjee Divakaruni's (1995) collection of short stories are indeed enticing, immediately drawing diasporic readers in. However, I am troubled by the organization of the gendered short stories under the metanarrative of "arranged marriage." Like the tensions in Samina Ali's work, I discover two themes: Choosing between family obligations—read as passive—or falling in love—read as agentic. The short stories "The Word Love" and "The Bats" may be the most illuminating.

Divakaruni, in "The Word Love" (57–72), creates a tale about an immigrant, Hindu-Bengali woman living in California with her white, American boyfriend (yet another reductive story of assimilation). They purchase a "sagging sofa ... together at a Berkeley garage sale" (57) and the woman is often curled up on this sofa crying because she cannot tell her mother about her relationship. She is torn between a mother who will not understand:

> You practice them out loud for days in front of the bathroom mirror, the words with which you'll tell your mother [in Calcutta] that you're living with a man. Sometime[s] the words are of confession and repentance. Sometime[s] they are angry, defiant. Sometimes they melt into a single, sighing sound. Love. You let the water run so he [the boyfriend] won't hear you and ask what those foreign phrases [Bengali] you keep saying mean. ... You don't want to have to explain. (57)

And a boyfriend who does not understand:

> You tried to tell him about your mother, how she'd seen her husband's face for the first time at her wedding. How when he died, she had taken off her jewelry and put on a widow's white. ... She lives in a different world. Can't you see that? She's never traveled more than a hundred miles from the village she was born in; she's never touched a cigarette or alcohol even though she lives in Calcutta, she's never watched a movie. (58)

The protagonist in "The Word Love" finds herself unable to live in silence and soon informs her mother that she is living with a white, American man and about the prospect of her marrying this man. The woman is immediately disowned:

> All through the next month you try to reach her. You call. The ayah answers. She sounds frightened when she hears your voice. Memsaab has

told her not to speak to you, or else she'll lose her job. "She had the lawyer over yesterday to change her will. What did you do, Missy baba, that was so bad?" (65)

Herein lies one of the problematic themes in *Arranged Marriage*. Divakaruni describes love and dating under the subtext of "modern"—a luxury that South Asian women cannot afford—and in opposition to the family or "tradition." At the moment of the mother's denial of her only daughter's existence, Divakaruni, in further articulating the relationship between the Bengali immigrant woman and her white, American boyfriend, continues to draw upon the commonly understood relationship between "east" or South Asian/"west" or American as family/individuality:

At first he was sympathetic. He held you when you lay sleepless at night. "Cry," he said. "Get it out of your system." Then, "It was bound to happen sooner or later. You must have known that. ... You had to cut the umbilical cord sometime." You pulled away when he said things like that. What did he know, you thought, about families, about (yes) love. He'd left home the day he turned eighteen. He only called his mother on Mother's Day. (68)

Divakaruni consistently uses binary terms to express the theme of family throughout her story as a discursive mechanism in which to situate the protagonist within a desire for stereotypical Americanization that is predicated on South Asianness as the "Other" (Naber 2006, 89). That is, Divakaruni deploys a cultural nationalist logic that represents the categories of "South Asian" and "American" in oppositional terms (Naber 2006).

My second-generation Bengali American respondents show that the choice is not between love and family, nor is it about South Asianness versus Americannes. Rather, both Rita and Ronica demonstrate how they creatively fuse love and family obligations by highlighting their agencies in the arranged marriage process (see Chapter 8). Remember, they do so by agreeing to meet men through desi matrimonial advertisements, but the women determine the rules of the meeting process. Rita says:

I told my mom that my rules are probably different than most people['s] who agree to this process. I told her I did not want to exchange pictures because I don't want it to be based on looks. Second, I don't want them to only pick someone for me to meet based on their biodata. If I am going to give someone a chance, it is going to be everyone. This is not a job interview, and I am not going to date someone off their résumé.

And Ronica says,

> I don't have a specific [way of meeting people]. I told my mom after a
> lot of coercion that I would meet someone in an arranged setting. ... The
> main reason I fight against it is because my parents won't put an ad that
> is reflective of me. If they were to put down what is true, then I would be
> more into it. I don't want to meet some guy who is going to be like "Who
> the fuck is this?"

And, unlike the protagonist's mother who returns all the letters sent to her—
"Not accepted. Return to Sender" (69), Rupa's parents, while withdrawing tui-
tion support after discovering that she was dating a white, Christian, American
man and that they were living together in a campus apartment, continued to
call her to encourage her to leave her boyfriend. Simultaneously, Rupa also
managed to stay connected with her family while maintaining intimate ties
with her boyfriend. Then, the women in my fieldwork clearly point to complex processes around nationalism and other forms of identities by rupturing
dichotomies of Orientalism and "modernity": family obligations versus individual desires/arranged marriage versus love/traditional versus modern/South
Asian versus American. My research participants express themes of family,
gender, and sexuality multidimensionally.

Next, too often, domestic violence and women's inabilities to leave their abusers are seen as a direct consequence of the South Asian patriarchal arranged-
marriage system, coupled with the devaluation of South Asian women as both
citizens and human beings, or as Mohanty's Third World Woman (1988). In the
short story "The Bats" (1–16), the young female protagonist notices a bruise on
her mother's face:

> One morning when she was getting me ready for school, braiding my
> hair into the slick, tight pigtails that I disliked because it always hung
> stiffly down my back, I noticed something funny about her face. Not the
> dark circles under her eye. Those were always there. It was high up on
> her check, a yellow blotch with its edge turning purple. It looked like my
> knee did after I bumped into the chipped mahogany dresser next to our
> bed last month. (2)

A handful of pages into the story, the girl and her mother secretly leave Calcutta
indefinitely to live with the mother's uncle in his village home. Divakaruni
unfolds a wonderfully emotional relationship between the girl and her old
great uncle or "Grandpa-Uncle." Just as the girl begins to develop a twinkle

in her eyes—a twinkle she had lost while living at home in Calcutta where "things fell a lot when Father was around, maybe because he was so large" (2)— her mother was waiting for her on the porch with an envelope in her hands. She softly says, "It's from him. ... He wants us to come back. He promises it won't happen again" (11). Grandpa-Uncle falls to the steps and asks my mother, "How did he know where you were?" (11) The girl's mother defensively replies, "I wrote to him. ... I couldn't stand it, the stares and whispers of the women. ... The loneliness of being without him" (11–12). The girl and the mother return home to Calcutta, but they move whenever they must, return home, and then move again—the ongoing and vicious cycle of domestic violence appropriately wraps the end of the story.

The tale is far too real for many married women, and Divakaruni astutely draws upon the *Cycle of Violence* from tension to battering to honeymoon (Shepard and Pence 1999). But are "western" women less tolerant of domestic violence than South Asian women? A vast number of studies show that spousal abuse supersedes racial, class, and cultural boundaries; domestic violence is just as much a problem among Americans as among South Asian women (Bergen 1998; Shepard and Pence 1999, Abraham 2000). Domestic violence does not happen in a vacuum, and the experience of domestic violence simply cannot be organized under one overarching narrative, such as arranged marriage. Doing so only serves to reinforce common stereotypes about South Asian women—exotic/erotic, passive/demure, dutiful/reserved, manipulative/calculative, asexual/frigid, traditional/old fashioned, conservative/politically unaware, dependent/faithful, inarticulate/ incompetent, loud/stupid, and slavish/subservient (Dasgupta and Warrier 1997)—rendering South Asian women's tolerance of battering as passivity, deep repression, and denial.

Without a doubt, Divakaruni probes numerous themes that are relevant to many South Asian women's lives. The award-winning fiction is well-written, thoughtful, and entertaining and presents numerous moments of intense identification between the characters and South Asian women readers (especially Hindu Bengali women). However, Divakaruni fails to overcome the stereotype of passive South Asian women and leaves her characters with little or no room to express agency. Moreover, Divakaruni describes several thematic issues in *Arranged Marriage* that simultaneously affect American (read as "white" and "western") women. Perhaps in different permutations, the meta-concepts of marriage and family obligations are everyday struggles for white women also (Hochschild and Machung 1990).

Indeed, the scope of Divakaruni's collection of stories was not meant to encompass gendered forms of whiteness, but, like Samina Ali, Divakaruni also traps South Asian women into a monolithic Third- World Woman stereotype.

Arranged Marriage provides a solid platform in which to render arranged marriage as a traditional, patriarchal, and "backward" practice—a singular and monolithic pedagogy. The overall message Divakaruni conveys is that arranged marriage is an intrusive practice, and the end results are that South Asian women are cloaked by tradition; women are trapped in loveless marriages; and there are stark, irreconcilable differences between women's individual desires and their family obligations. Divakaruni jettisons the opportunity of structural change in the marriage system, effacing the potential of arranged marriages for many South Asians, including the second-generation in America.

3   Tanuja Desai Hidier's *Born Confused*

Tanuja Desai Hidier (2002) offers another banal ABCD culture-clash discourse in *Born Confused* to enshroud the coming of age and self-discovery of a second-generation South Asian-American woman, Dimple Lala. With great nostalgia, Hidier beautifully captures desi meals of "[S]pinach with nymph-finger cloves of garlic ... a vat of cucumber *raita,* the two percent yoghurt thickened with sour cream ... lamb curry, the pieces melting tenderly off the bone ... deep bowls of kheer, coronated with crush[ed] pistachios and strands of saffron" (76– 77). However, Hidier is unable to remove herself from an Orientalist cultural conquest by opening her debut and award-winning novel with Dimple in a breached position in her mother's womb:

> I guess the whole mess started around my birthday. Amendment: my first birthday. I was born turned around, and apparently was holding my head in my hand in such a way that resulted in twelve treacherous hours of painful labor for my mother to eject me. My mom said she imagined I was trying to sort out some great philosophical quandary. ... But I think that was a polite way of saying I looked like I didn't get it. Born backwards and clueless. In other words, born confused. (1)

Dimple's life ahead will consist of a series of events that will leave her feeling misplaced and confused.

Hidier richly describes the pain of going through adolescence in brown skin, with black-haired oily pigtails, and a *shalwar kameez*–wearing mother—all while having a beautiful and popular white, blond-haired best friend, Gwyn—in a white middle-class suburb of New Jersey. Like Samina Ali's protagonist Layla, Dimple does not fit into the white mainstream: "The day I wore my hair in braids everyone yelled *Hey, Pocahontas,* and did that ahh-baah- baah-baah lip-slap at recess. You would have gotten a perm soon after as well" (3). Here, Dimple uses the language of oppositional binaries to talk about her relationship with her best friend, Gwyn: "In our twosome, I was 'the other one'—you know, the one the boy doesn't remember two second[s] after delivering the pizza. The too-curvy, clumsy ... wall- flower" (2). As a result, Hidier develops a character oblivious to her Hindu-Indian cultural heritage. Unlike my respondents who are fluent in spoken Bengali, Dimple is unable to speak even broken Marathi:

> I didn't know enough [Marathi] to get me to the other side of the room. ... This was Dadaji's constant sore point with my parents ... how could they have been so cruel as to cut off their own flesh and blood from one another through this ultimate act of linguistic negligence? (13)

Like Layla, Dimple is yet another ABCD conundrum (86–89).

I am not attempting to discount the pains associated with being part of the American racial and ethnic landscapes as a South Asian-American. As a child of over-educated immigrant Bangladeshi- Muslim parents, I am far too aware of the "restrictions" involved growing up brown and Muslim in white, Christian, working-class suburban Green Bay, Wisconsin, and Elgin, Illinois. Neeta Puri (2004) shares a childhood memory of "Othering" in Indiana. Puri describes a conversation with her teacher in grade school after a violent attack on Sikhs in India in 1984:

> "Where is your Uncle Goor-teep from?"
> I realized that I was angry at her for mispronouncing his name and my name, but I didn't know what to do. After all, what does a brown child say to a white woman with authority?
> "467 Lakewood Avenue."
> "Well, I didn't hear anything about that or read it in the papers," she said. "Are you sure?"
> I looked at her angry, and said, "Yes, I'm sure." ... The teacher then asked, "Do you mean what happened in In- dee-yuh this past week?"
> "Maybe." I honestly wasn't sure. "Well, that's a completely different problem," she said, speaking slowly. Turning to the rest of the class, she said. "In-dee-yuh is a place where people are really wild. They kill each other all the time." (23)

Nevertheless, if we accept the conflation of modernity with America and tradition with South Asia, then it will be impossible to account for the various women's liberation movements in South Asia along with the struggles women in America face in keeping their families together.

While Hidier is successful in breaking away from the assimilationist model-minority epistemology at moments, she systematically uses the points of egress to support ontologies that serve to reify the meanings of arranged marriage à la Divakaruni versus America as the land of the free, the only place women can live their lives as they choose à la Ali. Consider the words of Kavita, Dimple's newly arrived cousin from India, as she shares her thoughts about Sangita, her soon-to-be-married sister:

> That's how this kind of marriage [arranged] works, Dimple. ... I've seen cases where it works out, though I suppose you never really know; the divorce rate is low in India, but so is the speaking-up rate when it comes to women (83). ... You know, Dimple, they say in the East you love the person you marry and in the West you marry the person you love. (85)

Positioning herself as representative of America and freedom and in opposition to her sister Sangita, who is India and trapped, Kavita keeps on with her analysis:

> I guess all this talk about the wedding just made me a little sad. ... My life is so unlike Sangita's. ... I just worry sometimes that my sister has a lot of pressure on her because of my behavior. ... It's ... not staying in India and meeting a nice boy and not getting too overqualified to be a perfect wife. Which is exactly what Sangita's doing: settling in Mumbai and giving up on half her interests. (82–83)

Dhingra (2007) brings focus to the issue here:

> So much of the discourse on ethnicity ... refers to American culture as modern and as prioritizing the individual relative to a traditional and constraining immigrant heritage. This discursive dichotomy conceals the cultural conservatisms found in America, including the constraints placed on women and the rise of overt religiosity. Yet Asian Americans themselves often interpret their experiences within this framework. (2–3)

The redundant binary family versus love and obligatory sacrifices versus independence and individuality logic becomes a central discursive mechanism to understand essentialized cultural representations of India and America and this is embedded in the popular imaginations of both diasporic and mainstream readers. Hidier stubbornly continues to use Kavita as a medium that ignores the specificities of race, gender, culture, religion, class, and immigration. Kavita's entry into American higher education provides her with a venue in which to reject an arranged marriage and foster a meaningful lesbian relationship. While an immigrant identity may take a back seat in queer spaces, queers of color are ignored, feared, or fetishized in the U.S. As a queer Hindu Bengali American woman, Ronica recounts how her "coming out" process was framed within the confines of a Eurocentric sexual agenda (see Chapter 9):

> When I first came out as being queer, I felt excluded from the queer community because I didn't really know Asian people, South Asian people, or people of color that were queer ... The dominant discourse in the queer community is based around white people and that's really alienating ...

Ronica points to her concerns with queer diasporic South Asians lacking a safe place to articulate their cultures. Ronica problematizes the powerful role of the white gaze in queer activism and theory. Indeed, in the context of assimilation, queer immigrants have had to think through their cultural, political, religious, and sexual identities.

Next, Hidier effaces the importance of rupturing heteronormativity by using Kavita's lesbian partnership to mark arranged marriage as an oppressive act, a daughter's obligation to her family as superseding her own desires and living in America means that *all* women can realize their dreams. Unlike some of the women in my study who participated in arranged marriages, Dimple describes her potential mate, Karsh Kapoor, as a geeky computer scientist from India—"If he had a marital ad, it would have said this: 'strikingly average guy seeks fashion consultant'" (102)—and refuses to entertain the relationship any further. Rita, on the other hand says, "We talked for two and a half hours ... We talked about not very generic things. It was almost like we had known each other ... I had kind of felt something" (see Chapter 8). Through Dimple, Hidier labels South Asia and South Asians as "backward": "I'd rather stay home and contemplate the missing socks in the dryer than hit the town for a supposedly wild night out (not) with what was sure to be a bunch of uncle[s] and aunties" (149). The culture clash discourse draws on Orientalist descriptions of gendered South Asian cultural norms, implying that there is a single way a marriage can be arranged—lack of choice—and there is a single type of man to be married off to—a husband who controls his wife's time, space, and body.

Dimple soon discovers Karsh's alter ego, a DJ at a New York City club. Hidier astutely describes the New York City bhangra scene, connecting with Prashad's (2000) and Maira's (2002) findings. Hidier examines the nightclubs as spaces that break down the South Asia/America duality as Dimple explores the remix parties and finds new ways to (re-)negotiate her cultural identity. Karsh confides in Dimple: "That's what I love about clubs. ... It's all about the dynamic—music plays the people and people play the music. ... You're not alone. Your story, our families. It's yours, it's mine" (181). Here, on one hand, Hidier, like my respondent Rita, subverts the arranged marriage stereotype by breaking down Dimple's preconceptions of Karsh—Dimple discovers that he is not a "geek," but a DJ in an alternate cultural space. However, on the other hand, Dimple finds Karsh attractive and desirable because he is now in a role that her parents would disapprove of and never expect of Karsh—"the most unsuitable suitable boy" (95). Karsh no longer represents "backward" India, but, rather, Dimple finds him to be a progressive "Americanized" Indian. In other words, South Asian-American culture is localized in an imagined "true" South Asian culture that erupts out of the official discourses of U.S. state and corporate media and the notion of a universalized abstract American citizen (hegemonic U.S. nationalism), the pressures of assimilation, and the gendered racialization of South Asian women (and men) (Naber 2006, 88). Indeed, the Oriental phantasmatic is vibrantly alive. In the end, while Hidier does not wholly render arranged marriage as static and, in some instances, welcomes the potential of arranged marriages for second-generation South Asian-American women, she does so within the context of American modernity.

We need now to turn to Pulitzer-prize winner Jhumpa Lahiri and her novel *The Namesake* (2003).

4   Jhumpa Lahiri's *The Namesake*

Like Hidier, Jhumpa Lahiri is certainly sagacious in capturing the nuances of both the South Asian immigrant and Hindu-Bengali life in America, from lunch and dinner parties with chingri maacher kofta or shrimp cutlets swiftly lifted up from hot oil and left to rest in disposable foiled trays—"The families drop by at one another's homes on Sunday afternoons. They drink tea with sugar and evaporated milk and eat shrimp cutlets fried in saucepans" (38)—to the assumption that all South Asians are related to each other to some degree—the protagonist Gogol Ganguli's kindergarten principal Candace Lapidus "Shakes Ashoke's [Gogol's dad's] hand and tells him that there are two other Indian children at the school, Jayadev Modi in third grade and Rekha Saxena in fifth. Perhaps the Ganguli's know them" (57).

Lahiri also deeply entangles the reader with the notion of assimilation, the pains of growing up brown in white suburbia. Gogol, like the women who chose to participate in my study, simply wanted to be an unmarked American. After boarding a flight to return home to Boston from a family trip to India, Gogol experiences relief:

> He knows his mother will sit silently. ... But for Gogol, relief quickly replaces any lingering sadness. .... [He] asks the British Airways steward-ess for a glass of orange juice. With relief he puts on his headset to watch The Big Chill and listen to top- forty songs all the way home. (87)

Nupur Chaudhury's (2004) remark is relevant here:

> When I was younger, I used to forget that I was Indian. I used to think that being Indian never came up for me. I now realize that I didn't let it come up for me. I would never search from my Indian-ness. I realize now that what I would do was push it away. I never found my Indian-ness to be of any importance. (34)

I can still remember my own sense of relief boarding a flight from Dhaka-Zia International Airport to Chicago O'Hare International Airport and tearing open a packaged meal that would not make my stomach do acrobatic flips. The packaged meal was symbolic. It served to reestablish my Americanness and minimize my South Asianness.

My own field-studies show that the onset of early adulthood proves to be a turning point for many South Asians, where they could no longer amputate their heritage from their sense of self. Once again, Chaudhury (2004) provides critical insight:

> I returned to my private school for my senior year with a different out-look. I threw out the school's required summer reading list, and in its place I invented my own. A summer reading list full of books that I could relate to. As an Indian. As a Hindu. ... My self-imposed reading list was full of books that pertained to me .... (37)

Similarly, the women in my study argue that they began to develop a strong sense of cultural self as they entered early adulthood, a critical difference compared to their childhoods. Several women began to rework their "Otherness" through personal self- projects that served to awaken their desi pride. Noopur says: "At one time, I almost did shun being Indian. And I took that approach for a very long time. It was probably in college when I made [desi] friends and I realized that I do have this culture in me, and I do enjoy being who I am and being able to express it." Sinha (1998) finds that groups in college settings actively solicit members and try to build community by emphasizing a collective history and common issues based on experiences in the United States. Clearly, my respondents chose to abide by family expectations and develop pride in their cultural heritage and practices.

Lahiri's Gogol, on the contrary, quietly suffers a lifelong identity crisis. Lahiri imaginatively uses Gogol's name as the vehicle in which to take her readers through his journey of cultural and self-conflict as an ABCD, an identity that, one may argue, is pathological. When Gogol was born, his parents Ashima and Ashoke Ganguli did not have a name ready for him at the hospital in Cambridge, Massachusetts; Ashima and Ashoke were patiently waiting for a letter from India, which contained an auspicious name for the Gangulis' firstborn. The letter never arrived.

On the last day of the Gangulis' stay at the hospital, Ashoke chooses a temporary name to put on the birth certificate, "Gogol." While Gogol's name is legally "Gogol," his family considers it to be his dak naam or nickname and his bhalo naam or formal name to be Nikhil. Gogol hates his name because it has nothing to do with who he is. Gogol thinks his name is absurd and obscure— neither Indian nor American. When Gogol discovers that he is named after the Russian author Nikolai Gogol, he feels even more disconnected from his life: "He hates having to [sic] living with it. With a pet name turned good name, day after day, second after second. ... What dismays him most is the irrelevance of it all" (76).

A tension and conflict that arises between Gogol and his alter ego, Nikhil, becomes a persistent theme in the novel, serving as a paradigm of the ABCD construct. After his SATs, Gogol meets up with some friends to drive up to a college party. Gogol meets a girl there:

> But he doesn't want to tell Kim his name. He doesn't want to endure her reaction, to watch her lovely blue eyes grow wide. He wishes there were another name he could use ... But then he realizes there's no need to lie. ... He remembers the other name that had once been chosen for him, the one that should have been. "I'm Nikhil," he says for the first time in his life. (95–96)

Gogol legally changes his name from Gogol Ganguli to Nikhil Ganguli before his freshman year at Yale is about to begin (97):

> There is only one complication: he doesn't feel like Nikhil. Part of the problem is that the people who now know him as Nikhil have no idea

that he used to be Gogol. ... Even more startling is when those who normally call him Gogol refer to him as Nikhil. (105–106)

Lahiri's conceptual framework—the fantasy of assimilation—is explicitly revealed and clarified shortly after the name-change takes place:

Gogol has never heard the term ABCD. He eventually gathers that it stands for "American-born confused deshi." In other words, him. He learns that C could also stand for "conflicted." He knows that deshi, a generic word for "countryman," means "Indian," knows that his parents and all of their friends always refer to India simply as desh. He thinks of it as Americans do, as India. (118)

Lahiri simply ignores the long and problematic process of South Asian immigration and the fact that the second-generation has found the promises of unmarked citizenship elusive at best. Mohanty (1993) writes, "An American passport can open many doors. However, just carrying an American passport is no insurance against racism and unequal and unjust treatment within the U.S." (354). In this context, it is difficult to understand the ease with which Bharati Mukherjee claims that she is "American" (Visweswaran 1993, Grewal 1994).

Years later, Ashoke explains to his son how his name, Gogol, came to be. Ashoke survived a deadly train accident on the way to Jamshedpur in his early twenties; he was reading Nikolai Gogol's *The Overcoat* at the time. Ashoke was one of the few mangled survivors among hundreds of dead passengers lying on the West Bengal countryside (123). As Ashoke revisits "the night that had nearly taken his life, and the book that had saved him, and the year afterward, when he'd been unable to move" (123), Gogol sits there, "struggling to absorb the information, feeling awkward, oddly ashamed, at fault" (124). Gogol once again feels confused about his name: "And suddenly the sound of his name, uttered by his father as he has been accustomed to hearing it all his life, means something completely new, bound up with a catastrophe he has unwittingly embodied for years" (124).

Does Gogol embody his father's potential death or Ashoke's life that followed? The ongoing back-and-forth identification between the two names indicates Gogol's state of mind, his sense of self, and his connection (or lack thereof) to his heritage.

Gogol continues to feel empty, confused, and disconnected from his own life until his parents reintroduce him to a childhood friend, Moushoumi, as a potential marriage partner. Gogol, while hesitant about meeting Moushoumi under the pressures of marriage, immediately conjures up warmth during their initial meeting at a small local bar in Manhattan: "He struggles but fails to recall her presence at Pemberton Road; still, he is secretly pleased that she has seen those rooms, tasted his mother's cooking, washed her hands in the bathroom, however long ago" (200). Gogol can share things with Moushoumi that he has never been able to share with any other woman. Like many of my respondents, Gogol feels great comfort in being able to talk about pujas, mishti or sweets, and share secrets in public by speaking in Bengali with Moushoumi. The intimate relationship between Gogol and Moushoumi provides some hope to readers in that Gogol will be able to redeem himself from his cultural identity crisis. But Lahiri quickly dismisses Gogol and Moushoumi's arranged courtship and marriage as a function of ontological security rather than love: "They had both acted on the same impulse, that was their mistake. They had both sought comfort in each other, and in their shared world, perhaps for the sake of novelty, or out of the fear that that world was slowly dying" (284). Near the end of the novel, Moushoumi has an affair, and their marriage breaks apart: "[H]e wonders how he's arrived at all this: that he is thirty-two years old, and already married and divorced. His time with her seems like a permanent part of him that no longer has any relevance, or currency. As if that time were a name he'd ceased to use" (284). The protagonist Moushoumi is another redundant, monolithic ABCD. Moushoumi simply falls short in addressing the gendered nature of culture in the South Asian diaspora:

> Immersing herself in a third language [at Brown], a third culture, had been her refuge—she approached French, unlike things American or Indian, without guilt, or misgiving, or expectation of any kind. It was easier to turn her back on the two countries that claim her in favor of one that had no claim whatsoever. (214)

Perhaps this repression was a liberty Lahiri thought she could allow by constructing a male character at the center of the novel. Unlike the linear teleology followed by Gogol and Moushoumi, the women, my fieldwork attests, break apart the ABCD conundrum and reject models of assimilation along with ethnic enclave identity models. The question is not about assimilation, ethnic enclaves, or anything in between. Rather, the question lies in the ways South Asian-Americans collapse the one-dimensional multicultural model by producing multiple identities simultaneously, validating the categories that define human visibility as well as invisibility. *The Namesake,* along with the other texts critically reviewed here, represents South Asia within tropes of western hegemonic structure (Grewal 1993, 226–36).

CHAPTER 11

Contesting the Unitary Self

The ABCD Conundrum and Sites of Intervention

American Orientalism functions as hierarchical and mutually exclusive binary either/or categorical code: "[A] strict relationship of black and white, good and bad, and us and them is established" (Pigg 1996, 163–64; Jain 2005, 2). American Orientalist discourse is perhaps characteristic of the mindset of anorexics and bulimics who are obsessed "with maintaining a rigidly bounded self" (Zerubavel 1991, 51). Those who do not fit the oppositional scheme—the hybrid—are "excluded even from simple exclusion" (Jain 2005, 2). The women in my fieldwork show Orientalist descriptions are not adequate in explaining their lives. Kim's (1982) view of American-born Asians[1] is insightful:

> For the American-born Asian, the "choice" between Asia and America was false because it was in reality a choice between yellow and white. When "Asia" was chosen, it was because "American," or white doors seemed closed. Even the superficially practical solution to this externally imposed cultural conflict, suggested frequently by social psychologists ... was a false one because it assumes permanent and immutable inferiority to whites on the basis of race. (58)

Jain (2005) reasons concepts—like ambiguity—originally related to the marginalized became core concepts, and thus the discourse of difference itself works as a dispositive—"a repressive (power) structure that governs and excludes" (1). Spivak (1988) argues the traditional ways of reading texts and the traditional canon of knowledge leave out many important voices from "Other Worlds." The static composite identity of "South Asian" as a group is certainly an erroneous one because our identities, and identities in general, are continuously shaped and defined contextually. Brekhus (2003) writes of his respondents, "One's grammatical treatment of gay identity (and I will posit, of other identities) is seldom static ..." (136). My research participants' formations of their identities (both individual and collective) demand flexibility rather than following strict scripts. In identity work, the idea of mobility translates into

---

1   Kim's research focuses mainly on Chinese, Japanese, and Filipino communities in the U.S.

having many faces and facets instead of being limited to a fixed role/identity (Jain 2005, 3).

What should we learn from my respondents then, and how should it influence im/migration studies as well as other fields of relevance in the academy? First, I find the theme of identity and shifting identity best captures the class of events described in this research, and, second, marginality and difference are powerful spaces in which identities are produced. The research pinpoints how individuals intentionally and deliberately use culture in their everyday practices and interactions to construct, negotiate, and respond to their racialized ethnic identities (Jones 2001, 7). At large, I learn there is a growing need for academic departments to become increasingly integrated to better understand the world's political, social, and economic issues that maintain the hegemonic cultural and economic hierarchy.

1   Dissenting Spaces and the Changing Landscape of Otherness

1.1   *Lesson 1: Identity Grammar and Shifts*
My informants' experiences are certainly race-, class-, gender-, and nation-specific negotiations of a transnational experience of crafting an ethnocultural and national identity. While my ethnographic grounded theory remains close to the data throughout the research process, I do not eschew broad theoretical questions for narrower substantive questions (Brekhus 2003). My interviews determine that identity is the issue that best captures the class of events, and I focus on broader theoretical or epistemological concerns of identity, identity grammar, and shifts in identity grammar (Brekhus 2003).

The data captures social space varies by the configuration and exclusivity of the groups occupying it, space may be subdivided for social purposes and framed in boundaries such that the boundaries provide configurations for experience and interaction, and, localizing of social interaction in space influence social formations (Simmel 1950; Lechner 1991). Hence, there are contentious debates and disputes over the "proper" way to "perform" South Asian, American, and South Asian American identities. My respondents, like many of the suburban gay men in Brekhus's study, do identity as a verb and value "identity mobility." The women in this study exhibit what Brekhus (2003) would categorize as "commuter" or "chameleon." As adults, the women can move in and out of different identities and fit into multiple social contexts. The women's comments demonstrate there is far less coherence among their social groups and less uniformity in their worldviews compared to the ABCD archetype. I, therefore, do not attempt to develop a general theory from a specific ethnographic case (in the tradition of Goffman (1967, 1973, 1986) because much like Frankenberg (1994) and Jones (2001), I find few women can simply draw on one discursive repertoire to understand their identities. My interviewees move through discourses in which they criticized American Orientalism at one moment to expressions of pride in being American and "western") at another.

The research showcases the South Asian Diaspora in America is segregated by race and ethnicity and fragmented through binary conceptualizations of nation, class, sexuality, and gender, and my research participants reconstitute boundaries in enabling ways within the contemporary South Asian American context. The women selectively accept and maintain certain definitions, while rupturing others. The women in this study are both insiders and outsiders confronting community formations like Simmel's (1950) social type "the stranger": "The stranger ... is an element of the group itself. [Their] position as a full-fledged member involves both being outside it and confronting it" (402). The women's stories, in concurrence, resist essentialist and racialized notions of what it means to be both South Asian and American in America. Simmel (1950) would argue this is their assigned position by virtue of specific interactive relations (402–408): "[They] imports qualities into [the group], which do not and cannot stem from the group" (402). An intriguing theme emerges from the empirical story: Conflict has important implications for social identity. Bauman (2004) writes, "In each and every place I was—sometimes slightly, at some other times blatantly—'out of place'" (12). Conflict is broadly integral to general identity theory development, and it is often a result of exposure to more than one community of ideas and principles at a time (Bauman 2004, 12–13). Bauman (2004) comments, "[F]inding identity to be a bunch of problems rather than a single-issue campaign is a feature I share with a much greater number, practically with all men and women of the 'liquid modern 'era'" (12). While the experiences of my respondents are unique, their comments are not analytically distinct. The peculiarities of the women's biographies dramatize the fragmented nature of identity, or the trouble most of us have with resolving *la mêmeté* ("the sameness," the consistency and continuity of our identity over time) (Bauman 2004, 13). The interviewees share stories of vexing dilemmas and haunting choices that make "identity" a grave and controversial concern. Bauman (2004) writes, "Identity-seekers invariably face the daunting task of 'squaring a circle'" (10) and "'belonging' and 'identity' are not cut in rock, and they are not secured by a lifelong guarantee, that they are eminently negotiable and revocable ..." (11). Bauman teaches us that one must make choices, make them repeatedly, revise choices already made on another occasion, and reconcile contradictory and incompatible demands. Like Bauman's struggles with his national identity (9–10), my informants deal with identity as a task to be performed, and to be performed repeatedly rather than in a "one-off fashion" (12). The more one practices the skills needed to get by in ambivalent situations, the less overwhelming the challenges become (Bauman 2004, 13–14). The women demonstrate they are wholly or in part everywhere![2]

1.2   *Lesson 2: Marginality as a Space of Power*

My research participants' possibilities of producing their identities within Otherness (i.e., desiness) and normativeness (i.e., whiteness) simultaneously indicate a (historical) shift in identity and difference and center and periphery. In Brooks' (2002 study on unionization struggles in the garment industry, the testimony of Judith Viera, an El Salvadorian garment workers disport raced and cultured bodies as the driving force of the labor campaign. My point is the binary relation of Us and Other(s) no longer works well. Jain (2005) writes,

> There exist multiple hierarchies in the (everyday) practice of differentiation, and the construction of otherness in this day and age occurs in a complex situation of manifold uncertainties and ambivalence: clear, binary differences disappear, and, we, therefore, have to carefully (re-)map the new landscape of difference. (1)

The shift in the relationship between identity and Otherness, in effect, means Otherness must be constructed in different ways.

The historical shifts in an ever-changing global economy do not mean, however, concepts in the social sciences used to study Otherness and difference are no longer valuable. Brooks (2002) research displays despite a "successful" labor campaign, the women working in the garment factory in El Salvador had few alternative ways to participate in or contest the politics of the workplace.[3] Chakrabarty (2000) finds the universals propounded by the European Enlightenment remain indispensable to any social critique that seeks to

---

2   The generic analytic lens of identity transcends the specific factual content and context of the twenty-five second-generation South Asian American women I was studying (identity distinctions are not only important to my informants, but I would argue, also to Protestants or Democrats, for example). Since "South Asian" is a salient marked ethno-racial attribute within the context of U.S. immigration laws, South Asian American women are more aware of the way they manage their identities across time and space. They are perhaps an ideal case study for identity management. My informants reveal the identity management is not a uniquely second-generation South Asian American enterprise.

3   Said (2001) was acutely aware of the pervasive power of imperialism as one of the major causes of globalization. So too, Brooks (2002) argues that multinational corporations or MNCs are the masters of the new imperialism in a globalizing world.

address issues of social justice and equity. I take this to mean we are not a witness to a simple reversal in the relations of identity, Otherness, and difference. My interviewees expose similar modes of exclusion are at play, but the images attached to categories have changed. The women's "double movements" (à la Polanyi) and multiple contradictory alliances challenge "*both* a system of rule *and* a system of knowledge and representation" (Massey 1999, 31). I find Soja's (1996) thoughts about space, place, city, region, and urban fabric insightful here. Focusing on the interplay between the concepts of "Firstspace" ("the directly experienced world of empirically measurable and map[p]able phenomena" (17)) and "Secondspace" ("the 'conceived' space more concerned with images and representations of spatiality" (18)), Soja argues that the "spatiality of human life becomes passive ... two terms are never enough to deal with the real and imagined world" (19–20). Soja suggests a third possibility: "The ['Thirdspace'] works to break down the categorically closed logic of the 'either-or' in favor of a different, more flexible and expansive logic of the 'both-and-also'" (20). I find the Thirdspace (or the "Other") breaks down the way we look at things, the way we perceive them, and the way we seek to understand the spatiality of human life. The difference between thinking about Orientalist stories spatially and a-spatially is considerable and significant (Massey 1999, 28). This book calls for a need to construct identity in relation to an occupied space and vis-à-vis categories like gender, generation, class, race, regional distinctions, etc. (Brady 2002) to uncover how the women I interviewed create and enact racial, ethnic, class, gender, sexual, cultural, and nation categories, and how the identity categories become a crucial tool for managing the women's lives. In evaluating the women's stories, what I hope to offer is a conception of difference not as a fixed category, but as certain relation (Douglas 2001; Zerubavel 1991; Jain 2005), and a new (imaginary) hierarchy of difference based on the same old hierarchies.

Stonequist (1937) insists marginal persons often become pioneers and creative agents in a new social order. The women luminously reveal the significance and motives of culture and cultural change. Here, my respondents highlight the problems within "western" feminist discourse, and they connect with Mohanty's (1988) work on the instability of race, class, and gender. The women shatter the composite single Third World Woman by exhibiting the emergence of their own complex identities and cultural practices, adding to the mix of race, class, and gender liminality and practice. My interviewees shape their identities and develop complex experiences of authentic selves by refocusing their sense of self and identity in multiple ways and constructing what it means to be a South Asian woman in America. I highlight that marginality is a powerful space in which identities and culture are produced and consumed daily.

2   Becoming South Asian American (Over and Over Again)

The political, economic, and social processes that historically bind the "east"
and "west" (and "north" and "south") point to a process of cultural exchange
that occurs transatlantically through texts, readers, writers, and other critical
institutions. The intersections constitute a distinctive arena of cultural power
(Cohen and Dever 2002): The cultural displacement model plays a key role in
perpetuating the cultural authority of the "west." The ABCD archetype impli-
cates itself in the project of empire and consolidation of the American nation-
state. The chapters in this book intervene in this process by both vindicating
and challenging the imagined contours of the nation-state. The herstories of
the twenty-five women I interviewed whole heartedly propose a new approach
that criticizes and examines the boundaries implied in Orientalist dichotomies. Indeed, there is a call for broadening the range of "Others," highlighting
the various discourses deployed to construct "Otherness," and analyzing the
politics of difference (Sum 1999). How do we begin to renegotiate the boundaries of identity in order to encompass marginality and multiplicity? Going
beyond binary views of inside/outside or the politics of difference, Sum (1999)
argues, "Not only are there different types of other on the outside, there can
also be different types of other on the inside" (100). Like Brooks (2002, 2004,
2007), Puar (1993, 1994a, 1994b), and Jain (2005), Sum demands a continual
rearticulation of insider/outsider distinctions. The same discursive repertoire
of the hegemonic center remains of interest, but alternative accounts are considered by inverting the otherizing cultural categories and explanations promoted by the hegemonic center (101). The answer, therefore, is not to do away
with categories (Gerson and Peiss 1985).

The process of dividing is the initial step in making sense out of chaos
(Zerubavel 1991, 1). (Zerubavel (1991) points out, after all, the first three days
of the Creation were devoted to making distinctions!) Difference (and sim-
ilarity) exists between and among groups of people, and they have very real
consequences; difference simply cannot be erased. Second, a firm boundary
"makes it absolutely clear who is included in the group" by separating "them
from nonmembers" and helping "members develop a distinct collective identity;" boundaries "allow us to perceive any 'thing' at all" (Zerubavel 1991, 118).
Hence, the call is for "mutuality and interdependence replace oppositional
difference and exclusivity" (Puar 1994a, 27). I take this to mean an expansion
and blending of identity categories and spaces with dialectical and symbi-
otic relationships is not only appropriate but desperately needed. Flexible
social order is primary in creating fluid identity categories: "Flexible people
notice structures yet feel comfortable destroying them from time to time"

(Zerubavel 1991, 120). Meaning, the flexible mind challenges and defies any rigid classification system by being aware that any "thing" can be categorized in more than one mental context. Zerubavel (1991) writes, "Cow, for example, can be grouped together with both cat and corn as a word that begins with c, only with cat as a word that denotes animal, and only with corn as a word that denotes an edible object" (121). The point is the flexible mind promotes "plastic notion of meaning" by avoiding closure. While boundaries support the notion of separate spheres with distinct and uncrossable lines, the flexible mind suggests permeability and malleability of the lines. (It is precisely in a flexible socio-cognitive context that Gerson and Peiss (1985) develop and incorporate permeable boundaries in gender studies.) By concentrating on shifting and reshifting boundaries, it becomes possible to interpret and negotiate bodies outside of universalized experiences, reading bodies in multiple manners. Butler's (1997) performative as political strategy multiplies the sites of possible intervention:

> Performativity describes this relation of being implicated in that which one opposes, this turning of power against itself to produce alternative modalities of power, to establish a kind of political contestation that is not a "pure opposition" but a difficult labor of forging a future from resources inevitably impure. (241)

Opening the epistemological space for contestation from within the regime(s) of power, Butler makes possible feminist challenges to patriarchal authority in the terms and on the grounds of the authority itself. A flexible and fluid conception of what it means to be American and South Asian provides us with more viable choices. I reconnect with both Purkayastha (2005) and Maira (2002). The forty-eight interviewees in Purkayastha's study demonstrate they are both attached to heritage and celebrate reinvention of (new) traditions, often in the same temporal and spatial locations. Maira's in-depth, open-ended interviews with twenty-four Indian American college students lay out that the second-generation produces and participates in performances of culture that simultaneously remix elements of "tradition" and "modernity," "the authentic," and "the hybrid" (195). Maira (2002) and Purkayastha (2005) teach me the complex and contradictory experiences of the women in my research calls for a theory of identity in cultural practices that transcends old binaries of essentialization, while still encompassing both possibilities as aspects of the lived realities of social actors. I am inspired by poets, artists, writes, and performers who regularly participate in projects that give rise to diverse new voices like *Mango Tribe* (IL) and *Yoni Ki Baat* (CA).

As I approach my final words, the women in my fieldwork constructed diasporic identities that simultaneously assert a sense of belonging to the local-
ity in which they grew up while also proclaiming "difference," marking their
experiences of being an Other. Contrary to the clash of culture thesis, women
are not abandoning cultural traditions; rather, they are redefining them within
the contexts of both an imagined "true" South Asian culture and hegemonic
U.S. nationalism. Sandoval (1982) would argue a reconstituted understanding
of the women is based on a "self-conscious flexibility of identity" and not a
unitary sense of self (66). In this way, we can remind ourselves of Minh-ha's
(1991) description of becoming Asian American:

> Becoming Asian-American affirms itself at once as a transient and con-
> stant state: One is born over and over again ... rather than as fixed entity,
> thereby refusing to settle down in one (tubicolous) world or another. The
> ... condition certainly does not limit itself to a duality between two cul-
> tural heritages. (157)

My respondents are pushing up against the boundaries of old structures and
reconstitute the boundaries in more enabling ways. In this project, I set out
to explore what it means to be a second-generation South Asian American
woman. My interviewees actively engage with definitions of South Asianness and American-ness to reinterpret them, reject them, or reinvoke them.
The twenty-five women indicate being a South Asian American woman
means they (and I) live our lives within different, multiple, contradictory,
and complex experiences. What I have tried to offer in this book is a better
articulation of South Asian American ethnic theoretical perspectives, using
the perspectives as a case study to make larger comments on the nature of
identity. Like Mohanty (1988) and Anzaldúa (2001), I have tried to produce
an analysis that is politically focused and highly context-specific, mindful of
links between women and groups of women without falling into false gen-
eralizations and acknowledges both the contradictions and commonalities in women's experiences. This study demonstrates there is no one way to
exist as second-generation South Asian American women! In the aftermath
of the Trump Administration—willful government neglect and corporate
abuse—and the ongoing acts of xenophobia, ethnocentrism, jingoism, and
mass violence reverberating across Asian and South Asian and im/migrant
(un/documented) communities during the global pandemic, reconfiguring the
boundaries of identity may seem unfeasible and even unfathomable now. Ngai
(2004) writes, "Even as immigrants have become [a] larger and more visible
part of American society, alienage remains a conspicuous category of legal,

cultural, and political difference" (269). Nevertheless, our siblings in Palestine, Thailand, and Anishinaabe treaty land encourage us that it is at this moment of rigidity that survival and resilience should be mobilized. Together, the women's stories gloriously flash what it means to be human, what we are connected to, and what we are separate from.

References

Abraham, M. (2000). *Speaking the unspeakable: Marital violence among South Asian immigrants in the United States.* New Brunswick: Rutgers University Press.

Abu-Lughod, L. (2003). *Writing women's worlds: Bedouin stories.* Berkeley: University of California Press.

Agarwal, P. (1991). *Passage from India: Post-1965 Indian immigrants and their children: Conflicts, concerns, and solutions.* Palos Verdes: Yuvati.

Agnihotri, R. K. (1967). *Crisis of identity: The Sikhs in England.* New Delhi: Bahri.

Alba, R. (1992). *Ethnic identity: The transformation of white America.* Connecticut: Yale University Press.

Ali, S. (2004). *Madras on rainy days.* New York: Picador.

Ali, Z. (1993). Becoming agents of our identity." In the Women of South Asian Descent Collective (Eds.), *Our feet walk the sky: Women of the South Asian diaspora* (pp. 238). San Francisco: Aunt Lute.

Alvarez-Cáccamo, C. (1990). Rethinking conversational code-switching: Codes, speech varieties, and contextualization. *Annual Meeting of the Berkeley Linguistics Society, 16*(1), 16–19. https://doi.org/10.3765/bls.v16io.1716.

Aneesh, A. & Borocz, J. (2000). Logics of regimes of contingency: Total and relational closure define race and caste. Unpublished.

Anzaldúa, G. (2001). La conciencia de la mestiza: Towards a new consciousness. In K. Bhavnani (Editor), *Feminism and 'Race'* (pp. 93–107). New York: Oxford University Press.

Appadurai, A. (1990). Disjuncture and difference in the global cultural economy. *Public Culture, 2*(2), 1–24. https://doi.org/10.1215/08992363-2-2-1.

Badruddoja, R. (2008). Queer spaces, places, and gender: The tropologies of Rupa and Ronica. *Feminist Formations, 20*(2), 156–88.

Badruddoja, R. (2014). Third world woman, family, and marriage: South Asian diasporic fiction as a site for consolidation of the American nation-state. *South Asian Review, 35*(2), 81–104.

Bashi, V. (1998). Racial categories matter because racial hierarchies matter: A commentary. *Ethnic and Racial Studies, 21*(5), 959–968. https://doi.org/10.1080/01419879 8329748.

Bashi, V. (2001). Neither ignorance nor bliss: Race, racism, and the West Indian immigrant experience. In H.R. Cordero-Guzmán, R.C Smith, & R. Grosfoguel (Eds.), *Migration, transnationalism, and race in a changing New York* (pp. 212–238). Philadelphia: Temple University Press.

Bashi, V. & McDaniel, A. (1997). A theory of immigration and racial stratification. *Journal of Black Studies, 27*(5), 668–82.

Bauman, Z. (2004). *Identity*. Massachusetts: Polity.

Bellah, R., Madsen, R., Sullivan, W. M., Swidler, A., & Tipton, S.M. (1985). *Habits of the heart: Individualism and commitment in American life*. Berkeley: University of California Press.

Bergen, R. K. (Ed.). (1998). *Issues in intimate violence*. Los Angeles: Sage.

Bhabha, H. (1990). *Nation and narration*. London: Routledge.

Bhabha, H. (1994). *The location of culture*. London and New York: Routledge.

Brady, M.P. (2002). *Extinct land, temporal geographies: Chicana literature and the urgency of space*. Durham and London: Duke University Press.

Brah, A. (1996). *Cartographies of diaspora: Contesting identities*. London: Routledge.

Brekhus, W. (2003). *Peacocks, chameleons, centaurs: Gay suburbia and the grammar of social-identity*. Illinois: University of Chicago Press.

Brodkin, K. (1998). *How Jews became white folks and what that says about race in America*. New Brunswick: Rutgers University Press.

Brooks, E. (2002). The ideal Sweatshop? Gender and transnational protest. *International Labor and Working-Class History*, 61. https://doi.org/10.1017/S0147547902000078.

Brooks, E. (2004). Economy and the war on terror. *American Sociological Association Annual Meetings,* San Francisco, CA.

Brooks, E. C. (2007). *Unraveling the garment industry: Transnational organizing and women's work (social movements, protests and contention)*. Minneapolis: University of Minnesota Press.

Butler, J. (1991). Imitation and gender insubordination. In D. Fuss (Editor), *inside/out: Lesbian theories, gay theories* (pp. 13–31). New York: Routledge.

Butler, J. (1997). Performative acts and gender constitution: An essay on phenomenology and feminist theory. In K. Conboy, N. Medina, & S. Stanbury (Eds.), *Writing on the body: Female embodiment and feminist theory* (pp. 401–418). New York: Columbia University Press.

Butler, J. (1999). *Gender trouble*. New York and London: Routledge.

Byrne, A. (2000a). Researching one an-other. In A. Byrne & R. Lentin (Eds.), *(Re)searching women: Feminist research methodologies in the social sciences in Ireland* (pp. 140–166). Dublin, Ireland: Institute of Public Administration.

Byrne, A. (2000b). Singular identities: Managing stigma, resisting voices. *Women's Studies Review* 7, 13–24.

Byrne, A. (2003). Developing a sociological model for researching women's self and social identities. *European Journal of Women's Studies, 10*(4), 443–464. https://doi.org/10.1177/13505068030104010.

Census, Staff of United States Bureau of. 2000. "Census of Population and Housing." U.S. Bureau of Census.

Chakrabarty, D. (2000). *Provincializing Europe: Postcolonial thought and historical difference*. Princeton: Princeton University Press.

Chaudhury, N. (2004). A place where I want to be. In A. Han and J. Hsu (Eds.), *Asian-American x: An intersection of 21st century Asian-American voices*. Ann Arbor: University of Michigan Press.

Clough, P. T. (1998). *The end(s) of ethnography: From realism to social criticism*. New York: Peter Lang.

Cohen, M. & Dever, C. (2002). *The literary channel: The international invention of the novel*. Princeton and Oxford: Princeton University Press.

Collective, Kitchen Table (Eds.). (2000). *Bolo! Bolo! A collection of writings by second generation South Asians living in North America*. Canada: South Asian Professionals' Networking Association.

Collins, P. H. (2000). It's all in the family: Intersections of gender, race, and nation. In U. Narayna & S. Harding (Eds.), *Decentering the center* (pp. 156–176). Bloomington: Indiana University Press.

Collins, P. H. (2004). *Black sexual politics: African Americans, gender, and the new racism*. New York and London: Routledge.

Connell, R.W. (1995). *Masculinities*. Berkeley: University of California Press.

Conzen, K.N. (1991). Mainstreams and side channels: The localization of immigrant cultures. *Journal of American Ethnic History 10*, 5–20.

Cornell, S. & Hartmann, D. (1998). *Ethnicity and race: making identities in a changing world*. Thousand Oaks: Pine Forge.

Counihan, C. M. (2004). *Around the tuscan table*. New York and London: Routledge.

Crenshaw, K. (1991). Mapping the Margins: Intersectionality, identity politics, and violence against women of color. *Stanford Law Review, 43*(6), 1241. https://doi.org/10.2307/1229039.

Dasgupta, S. (1993). Glass Shawls and Long Hair. *Ms. 3*(5), 76.

Dasgupta, S. D. (1989). *On the train of an uncertain dream: Asian Indian immigrant experience in America*. New York: AMS.

Dasgupta, S. D. & Warrier, S. (1997). *In visible terms: Domestic violence in the Asian Indian context*. Union: Manavi.

Davis, F. J. (1991). *Who is Black? One nation's definition*. PA: Penn State University Press.

Désert, J. (1997). Queer Space. In G. B. Ingram, A. Bouthilette, & Y. Retter. (Eds.), *Queers in Space: Communities, Public Places, Sites of Resistance* (pp 17–26.). Seattle: Bay.

DeVault, M. L. (1999). *Liberating method: Feminism and social research*. Philadelphia: Temple University Press.

Dhingra, P. (2007). *Managing multicultural lives: Asian American professionals and the challenge of multiple identities*. Stanford: Stanford University Press.

Divakaruni, C. B. (1995). *Arranged marriage*. New York: Doubleday.

Douglas, M. (2001). *Purity and danger: An analysis of concepts of pollution and taboo*. Baltimore: Penguin.

Escoffier, J. (1991). The limits of multiculturalism. *Socialist Review, 3/4*.

Fanon, F. (1986). *Black skin, white mask.* London: Pluto.

Fisher, M.P. (1980). *The Indians of New York City: A study of immigrants from India.* New Delhi: Heritage.

Foucault, M. (1990). *The history of sexuality: An introduction.* New York: Vintage.

Foucault, M. (1994). *The order of things: The archeology of the human sciences.* New York: Vintage.

Foucault, M. (1995). *Discipline and punish: The birth of a prison* (2nd ed.). New York: Vintage.

Frankenberg, R. (1994). Whiteness and Americanness: Examining constructions of race, culture, and nation in white women's narratives." In R. Sanjek and S. Gregory (Eds.), *Race* (pp. 62–78). New Brunswick: Rutgers University Press.

Freeman, C. (2000). *High tech and high heels in the global economy: Women, work, and pink-collar identities in the Caribbean.* Durham: Duke University Press.

Ganguly, K. (2001). *States of exception: Everyday life and postcolonial identity.* Minneapolis: University of Minnesota Press.

Gans, H. (1979). Symbolic ethnicity: The future of ethnic groups and cultures in America. *Ethnic and Racial Studies 2,* 1–20.

Gecas, V. & Burke, P.F. (1995). Self and identity. In K.S. Cook, G.A. Fine, and J.S. House (Eds.), *Sociological Perspectives on Social Psychology* (pp. 41–67). Boston: Allen and Bacon.

Gerson, J.M & Peiss, K. (1985). Boundaries, negotiation, consciousness: Reconceptualizing gender relations. *Social Problems 32,* 317–31.

Gibson, M.A. (1988). *Accommodation without assimilation: Sikh immigrants in an American high school.* Ithaca: Cornell University Press.

Giddens, A. (1991). *Modernity and self-identity: Self and society in the late modern age.* Stanford: Stanford University Press.

Gillis, J. R. (1997). *A world of their own making: Myth, ritual, the quest for family values.* Cambridge: Harvard University Press.

Gilroy, P. (1995). *The Black Atlantic: Modernity and double consciousness.* Cambridge: Harvard University Press.

Glaser, B. G. (1992). *Basics of grounded theory analysis: Emergence vs. forcing.* Mill Valley, CA: Sociology.

Glaser, B. G. & Strauss, A. (1967). *The discovery of grounded theory.* Chicago: Aldine.

Goffman, E. (1967). *Interaction ritual: Essays on face-to-face behavior.* New York: Pantheon.

Goffman, E. (1973). *The presentation of self in everyday life.* New York: Overlook.

Goffman, E. (1986). *Stigma: notes on the management of spoiled identity.* New York: Simon & Schuster.

Gopinath, G. (2005). *Impossible desires: Queer diasporas and South Asian public cultures (perverse modernities).* Durham: Duke University Press.

Gordon, M. M. (1964). *Assimilation in American life: The role of race, religion, and national origins.* New York: Oxford University Press.

Grewal, I. (1993). Reading and writing the South Asian diaspora: Feminism and nationalism in North America. In the Women of South Asian Descent Collective (Eds.), *Our feet walk the sky: Women of the South Asian diaspora* (pp 226–236.). San Francisco: Aunt Lute.

Grewal, I. (1994). The Postcolonial, ethnic studies, and the diaspora. *Socialist Review (The Traveling Nation: India and Its Diaspora)* 24, 45–74.

Guglielmo, T. A. (2003). *White on arrival: Italians, race, color, and power in Chicago, 1890–1945.* New York and Oxford: Oxford University Press.

Gumperz, J. J. (1982). *Discourse strategies.* Cambridge: Cambridge University Press.

Gupta, A. (1998). *Postcolonial developments: Agriculture in the making of modern India.* Durham: Duke University Press.

Hankiss, A. (1981). Ontologies of the self: On the mythological rearranging of one's life-history. In D. Bertaux (Editor), *Biography and society: The life history approach in the social sciences* (pp. 203–209). Beverly Hills: Sage.

Hartmann, D. & Gerteis, J. (2005). Dealing with diversity: Mapping multiculturalism in sociological terms. *Sociological Review* 23, 218–40.

Hasnat, N. (1998). Being 'Amreekan': Fried chicken versus chicken tikka. In S. D. Dasgupta (Editor), *A patchwork shawl: Chronicles of South Asian women in America* (pp. 33–45). New Brunswick: Rutgers University Press.

Hidier, T. D. (2002). *Born confused.* New York: Scholastic.

Hing, B.H. (1993). *Making and remaking Asian America trough immigration policy, 1850–1990.* Stanford: Stanford University Press.

Hochschild, A. R., and Machung, A. (1990). *The second shift.* New York: William Morrow.

Hogg, M.A. (2001). Social-Identity and the sovereignty of the group. In C. Sedikides and M.B. Brewer (Eds.), *Individual self, relation self, collective self* (pp. 123–143). Ann Arbor: Taylor & Francis.

hooks, b. (1990). *Yearning: Race, gender and cultural politics.* Boston: South End.

hooks, b. (1992). *Black looks: Race and representation.* Boston: South End.

Hyun, J. (2005). *Breaking the bamboo ceiling: Career strategies for Asians.* New York: HarperCollins.

Ignatiev, N. (1995). *How the Irish became white.* New York and London: Routledge.

Ingram, G. B., Bouthillette, A. & Retter, Y. (1997). Lost in space: Queer theory and community activism at the Fin-de-Millénaire. In G. B. Ingram, A. Bouthilette, & Y. Retter (Eds.), *Queers in space: Communities, public places, sites of resistance* (pp. 3–16). Seattle: Bay.

Islam, N. (1993). In the belly of the multicultural beast, I am named South Asian. In the Women of South Asian Descent Collective (Eds.), *Our feet walk the sky: Women of the South Asian diaspora* (pp. 242–245). San Francisco: Aunt Lute.

Islam, N. (1998). Naming desire, shaping identity: Tracing the experiences of Indian lesbians in the United States. In S. D. Dasgupta (Editor), *A patchwork shawl: Chronicles of
South Asian women in America* (pp. 72–96). New Brunswick: Rutgers University Press.

Islam, S. (1993). Toward a global network of Asian lesbians. In R. Ratti (Editor), *A lotus
of another color: An unfolding of the South Asian gay and lesbian experience* (pp. 41–
46). Boston: Alyson.

Jain, A. (2005). Differences in difference: A cognitive mapping of the landscape of otherness. Conference Paper Presented in Edward Said and Orientalism at University
of Massachusetts, Boston.

Jenkins, R. (1996). *Social-identity*. New York and London: Routledge.

Jones, K. W. (2001). *Accent of privilege: English identities and Anglophilia in the U.S.*
Philadelphia: Temple University Press.

Kabeer, N. (2000). *The power to choose: Bangladeshi women and labour market decisions in London and Dhaka*. New York and London: Verso.

Kam, K. (2020, October 8). *Why domestic violence calls are surging for Asian American
women amid the pandemic*. NBCNews.com. https://www.nbcnews.com/news/
asian-america/why-domestic-violence-calls-are-surging-asian-american-women
-amid-n1240663.

Kawale, R. (2003). A kiss is just a kiss ... Or is it? South Asian lesbian and bisexual
women and the construction of space. In N. Puwar and P. Raghuram (Eds.), *South
Asian women in the diaspora* (pp. 181–199). Oxford and New York: Berg.

Kelly, J. (1998). *Under the gaze: Learning to be Black in white society*. Canada: Fernwood.

Khan, S. (1993). Khush, A SHAKTI Report. Camden: Camden Council.

Kibria, N. (1993). *Family tightrope: The changing lives of Vietnamese Americans.*
Princeton: Princeton University Press.

Kibria, N. (1998). The racial gap: South Asian-American racial identity and the
Asian-American movement. In L.D. Dhingra Shankar & R. Srikanth (Eds.), *A
part yet apart: South Asians in Asian America* (pp. 69–78). Philadelphia: Temple
University Press.

Kibria, N. (2002a). College and notions of 'Asian-Americans': Second-Generation
Chinese Americans and Korean-Americans. In P.G. Min (Editor), *Second generation: Ethnic identity among Asian-Americans* (pp. 183–208). New York: Altamira.

Kibria, N. (2002b). *Becoming Asian-American: Second-Generation Chinese and Korean-
American identities*. Baltimore and London: John Hopkins University Press.

Kim, E. H. (1982). *Asian-American literature: An introduction to the writings and their
social context*. Philadelphia: Temple University Press.

Kwong, P., & Miščević, D. (2005). *Chinese America: The untold story of America's oldest
new community*. New York: New Press.

Lahiri, J. (2003). *The namesake: A novel*. Boston: Houghton.

Lash, S., & Urry, J. (1994). *Economies of signs & space*. London, Thousand Oaks, and New Delhi: Sage.

Lechner, F. J. (1991). Simmel on social space. *Theory, Culture & Society, 8*(3), 195–201.

Lederach, J.P. (1995). *Preparing for peace: Conflict transformation across cultures*. Syracuse: Syracuse University Press.

Lentin, R. (2000). Constructing the self in narrative feminist research as auto/biography. In A. Byrne and R. Lentin (Eds.), *(Re)searching women: Feminist research methodologies in the social sciences in Ireland* (pp. 247–264). Dublin: Institute of Public Administration.

Leonard, K. I. (1992). *Making ethnic choices: California's Punjabi Mexican Americans*. Philadelphia: Temple University Press.

Leonard, K. I. (1997). *The South Asian-Americans*. Westport and London: Greenwood.

Lessinger, J. (1995). *From the Ganges to the Hudson: Indian immigrants in New York*. Boston: Allyn and Bacon.

Ludden, D. (2002). *India and South Asia: A short history (including Bangladesh, Bhutan, Nepal, Pakistan, and Sri Lanka)*. Oxford: Oneworld.

Maira, S. M. (2002). *Desis in the house: Indian American youth culture in New York City*. Philadelphia: Temple University Press.

Mani, B. (2003). Undressing the diaspora. In N. Puwar and P. Raghuram (Eds.), *South Asian women in the diaspora* (pp. 117–136). Oxford and New York: Berg.

Mani, L. (1993). Gender, class and cultural conflict: Indu Krishnan's knowing her place. In the Women of South Asian Descent Collective (Eds.), *Our feet walk the sky: Women of the South Asian Diaspora* (pp. 32–36). San Francisco: Aunt Lute.

Mankekar, P. (1994). Reflections on diasporic identities: A prolegomenon to an analysis of political bifocality. *Diaspora* 3.

Massey, D. (1999). Imagining globalization: Power-Geometrics of time-space. In A. Brah, M.J. Hickman, & M. Mac an Ghaill, *Global futures: Migration, environment and globalization* (pp. 27–44). New York: St. Martin's.

Massey, D. (2002). *Beyond smoke and mirrors: Mexican immigration in an era of economic integration*. New York: Russell Sage Foundation.

Mauthner, N. & Doucet, A. (1998). *Feminist dilemmas in qualitative research: Public knowledge and private lives*. London: Sage.

McCall, G. L. & Simmons, J.L. (1966). *Identities and interactions* (revised edition). New York: Free Press.

McCall, L. (2001). *Complex inequality: Gender, class, and race in the new economy*. New York: Routledge.

McIntosh, P. (1988). White privilege and male privilege: A personal account of coming to see correspondences through work in women's studies. Working Paper for Wellesley College Center for Research on Women, Wellesley, MA.

Mead, G. H. (1962/1967). *Mind, self, and society* (C.W. Morris, Ed.). Chicago: University of Chicago Press.

Min, P. G. and Hong, J. (2002). Ethnic attachment among second-generation Korean-Americans. In P. Gap Min (Editor), *Second generation: Ethnic identity among Asian-Americans* (pp. 113–128). New York: Altamira.

Min, P. G. and Kim, R. (2002). Formation of ethnic and racial identities; Narratives of Asian-American professionals. In P. Gap Min (Editor), *Second generation: Ethnic identity among Asian-Americans* (pp. 53–84). New York: Altamira.

Minh-ha, T. (1989). *Women native other*. Bloomington: Indian University Press.

Minh-ha, T. (1991). *When the moon waxes red*. New York: Routledge.

Mirchandani, R. (2004). Postmodernism and sociology: From the epistemological to the empirical. *Sociological Theory, 23* (1).

Mirza, H. S. (1997). Introduction: Mapping a genealogy of Black British feminism. In H.S. Mirza (Editor), *Black British feminism: A reader* (pp. 1–30). London: Routledge.

Mohanty, C. T. (1988). Under Western eyes: Feminist scholarship and colonial discourses. *Feminist Review 30*, 65–88.

Mohanty, C.T. (1993). Defining genealogies: Feminist reflections of being South Asian in North America. In the Women of South Asian Descent Collective (Eds.), *Our feet walk the sky: Women of the South Asian diaspora* (pp. 351–358). San Francisco: Aunt Lute.

Mohanty, C. T. (2003). *Feminism without borders: Decolonizing theory, practicing solidarity*. Durham and London: Duke University Press.

Mukherjee, B. (1989). *Jasmine*. New York: Grove.

Mukherji, A. (2020). *South Asian domestic violence survivors in Silicon Valley grapple with COVID-19 lockdown*. The Wire. https://thewire.in/women/south-asian-domestic-violence-survivors-in-silicon-valley-grapple-with-covid-19-lockdown.

Mukhi, S.M. (2000). *Doing the Desi thing: Performing Indianness in New York City*. New York: Garland.

Naber, N. (2006). Arab American femininities: Beyond Arab virgin/american(ized) whore. *Feminist Studies, 32*(1), 87–111.

Nagel, J. (1994). Constructing ethnicity: Creating and recreating ethnic identity and culture. *Social Problems, 41*(1), 152–76.

Nagel, J. (2003). *Race, ethnicity, and sexuality: Intimate intersections, forbidden frontiers*. Oxford: Oxford University Press.

Narayan, U. (1997). *Dislocating cultures: Identities, traditions, and third world feminism*. New York and London: Routledge.

Narayan, U. (2000). Essence of culture and sense of history: A feminist critique of cultural essentialism. In U. Narayan & S. Harding, *Decentering the center* (pp. 88–100). Bloomington: Indiana University Press.

Ngai, M. N. (2004). *Impossible subjects: Illegal aliens and the making of modern America*. Princeton and Oxford: Princeton University Press.

Nippert-Eng, C. E. (1995/1996). *Home and work: Negotiating boundaries through every-day life*. Chicago: University of Chicago Press.

Omi, M. & Winant, H. (1986). *Racial formation in the United States: From the 1960s to the 1980s*. New York: Routledge.

Panjabi, K. (1997). Probing "morality" and state violence: Feminist values and communicative interaction in prison testimonios in India and Argentina. In M. J. Alexander & C. T. Mohanty (Eds.), *Feminist genealogies, colonial legacies, democratic futures* (pp.151–169). New York: Routledge.

Pigg, S. L. (1996). The credible and the credulous: The question of 'villager's beliefs' in Nepal. *Cultural Anthropology 11*, 160–201.

Polanyi, K. (1944). *The great transformation*. Boston: Beacon.

Poore, G. (1998). The language of identity. In S. D. Dasgupta, *A patchwork shawl: Chronicles of South Asian women in America* (pp.). New Brunswick: Rutgers University Press.

Portes, A. (1995). Economic sociology and the sociology immigration: A conceptual overview. In A. Portes, *The economic sociology of immigration: Essays on networks, ethnicity, and entrepreneurship* (pp. 1–41). New York: Russell Sage Foundation.

Portes, A. (1996). *The new second generation*. New York: Russell Sage Foundation.

Portes, A. & Rumbaut, R.G. (2001). *Legacies: The story of the immigrant second generation*. Los Angeles: University of California Press.

Prashad, V. (2000). *The karma of Brown folk*. Minneapolis: University of Minnesota Press.

Prashad, V. (2002). *Everybody was Kung Fu fighting: Afro-Asian connections and the myth of cultural purity*. Boston: Beacon.

Prashad, V. (2003). Bruce Lee and the anti-Imperialism of Kung Fu: A polycultural adventure. *Positions: East Asia Cultures Critique*, 11(1), 51–90.

Puar, J. (1993). Identity, racism and culture: Second-Generation Sikh women and oppositionally active 'whiteness.' Thesis Submitted for MA in Women's Studies, University of York, England.

Puar, J. (1994a). Resituating discourses of 'whiteness' and 'asianness' in Northern England. *Socialist Review, 1*(2), 21–54.

Puar, J. (1994b). Writing my way 'home': Traveling South Asian bodies and diasporic journeys. *Socialist Review (The Traveling Nation: India and Its Diaspora)* 24, 75–108.

Puar, J. (2004). Abu Ghraib: Arguing against exceptionalism. *Feminist Studies (The Prison Issue)*, 30(2), 522–34.

Puar, J. & Rai. A.S. (2002). Monster, terrorist, fag: The war on terrorism and the production of docile patriots." *Social Texts*, 20, 117–48.

Puri, N. (2004). 1984. In A. Han and J. Hsu (Eds.), *Asian-American X: An intersection of 21st century Asian-American voices*. Ann Arbor: University of Michigan Press.

Purkayastha, B. (2005). *Negotiating ethnicity: Second-Generation South Asian-Americans traverse a transnational world*. New Brunswick: Rutgers University Press.

Raghuram, P. (2003). Fashioning the South Asian Diaspora: Production and consumption tales. In N. Puwar & P. Raghuram (Eds.), *South Asian women in the diaspora* (pp. 67–86). Oxford and New York: Berg.

Ragin, C. C. (1994). *Constructing social research: The unity and diversity method.* Chicago: Pine Forge.

Ramji, H. (2003). Engendering diasporic identities. In N. Puwar & P. Raghuram (Eds.), *South Asian women in the diaspora* (pp. 227–242). Oxford and New York: Berg.

Rich, A. (1986). *Blood, bread, and purity: Selected prose, 1979–1985.* New York: W.W. Norton.

Rumbaut, R. G. & Portes, A. (2001). *Ethnicities: Children of immigrants in America.* Los Angeles: University of California Press.

Said, E. W. (1979). *Orientalism.* New York and Canada: Random House.

Said, E. W. (2001). *Power, politics, and culture.* New York: Pantheon.

Sandoval, C. (1982). Women respond to racism: A report on the national women's studies association conference, Storrs, Connecticut, 1981. Washington, D.C.: Center for Third World Organizing.

Sandoval, C. (1991). U.S. third world feminism: The theory and method of oppositional consciousness in the postmodern world. *Genders 10*, 1–24.

Shah, N. (1998). Sexuality, identity, and the uses of history. In D. Eng & A. Hom (Eds.), *Q & A: Queer in Asia America,* pp. 141–156. Philadelphia: Temple University Press.

Shah, S. (1997). *Dragon ladies: Asian-American feminists breathe fire.* Boston: South End.

Shamir, R. (2005). Without borders? Notes on globalization as a mobility regime. *Sociological Theory 23*, 197–217.

Shankar, R., and Srikanth, R. (Eds.). (1998). *A part yet apart: South Asians in Asian America.* Philadelphia: Temple University Press.

Shepard, M. F., and Pence, E. L. (Eds.). (1999). *Coordinating community responses to domestic violence: Lessons from Duluth and beyond.* Los Angeles: Sage.

Shohat, E. (1998). *Talking visions: Multicultural feminism in a transnational age* (E. Shohat, Ed.). New York: MIT Press.

Simmel, G. (1950). *The sociology of Georg Simmel* (K. Wolff, Trans.). Glencoe: Free Press.

Sinha, S. T. (1998). From campus to community politics in Asian America. In L. D. Shankar and R. Srikanth (Eds.), *A Part Yet Apart: South Asians in Asian America.* Philadelphia: Temple University Press.

Soja, E. (1996). *Thirdspace: Journeys to Los Angeles and other real-and-imagined places.* Cambridge and Oxford: Blackwell.

Song, M. (1998). Pakhar Singh's argument with Asian America: Color and structure of race formation. In L. D. Shankar & R. Srikanth (Eds.), *A part yet apart: South Asians in Asian America* (pp. 79–102). Philadelphia: Temple University Press.

Spivak, G. C. (1988). Can the subaltern speak? In C. Nelson and L. Grossberg (Eds.), *Marxism and the interpretation of culture* (pp. 271–316). Chicago: University of Illinois Press.

Stonequist, E. V. (1937). *The marginal man: A study in personality and cultural conflict.* New York: Charles Scribner's Sons.

Strauss, A. and Corbin, J. (1998). *Basics of qualitative research techniques and procedures for developing grounded theory.* Thousand Oaks: Sage.

Stryker, S. (1980). *Symbolic interactionism: A social structural version.* Menlo Park: Benjamin/Cummings.

Sum, N. (1999). New orientalisms, global capitalism, and the politics of synergetic differences: Discursive construction of trade relations between the USA, Japan and the East Asian NICs. In A. Brah, M.J. Hickman, & M. Mac an Ghaill, *Global futures: Migration, environment and globalization* (pp. 99–121). New York: St. Martin's.

Tajfel, H. (1981). *Human groups and social categories: Studies in social psychology.* New York: Cambridge University Press.

Twine, F. W. (1997). *Racism in a racial democracy: The maintenance of white supremacy in Brazil.* New Brunswick: Rutgers University Press.

Vargas, S.R.L. (1998). Deconstructing homo[geneous] americanus: The white ethnic immigrant narrative and its exclusionary effect. *Tulane Law Review, 72.*

Visweswaran, K. (1993). Predicaments of the hyphen. In the Women of South Asian Descent Collective (Eds.), *Our feet walk the sky: Women of the South Asian Diaspora* (pp. 301–319). San Francisco: Aunt Lute.

Visweswaran, K. (1994). *Fictions of feminist ethnography.* Minneapolis and London: University Minnesota Press.

Visweswaran, K. (1997). Diaspora by design: Flexible citizenship and South Asians in the U.S. racial formations. *Diaspora 6.*

Vogt, H. (1954). Language Contacts. *Word, 10*(2–3), 365–74.

Waters, M. C. (1990). *Ethnic options: Choosing ethnic identities in America.* Berkeley, Los Angeles, and London: University of California Press.

Waters, M. (1996). *Immigrant families at risk: Factors that undermine chances of success.* In A. Booth, A.C. Crouter, & N. Landale (Eds.), *Immigration and the family: Research and policy on U.S. immigrants* (pp. 79–90). New Jersey: Lawrence Erlbaum.

White, H. (1978). The historical text as literary artifact. In *Topics of Discourse: Essays in Cultural Criticism* (pp. 81–99). Baltimore: John Hopkins University Press.

Winant, H. (1994). *Racial conditions: Politics, theory, comparison.* Minneapolis: University of Minnesota Press.

Yegenoglu, M. (1998). *Colonial fantasies: Towards a feminist reading of orientalism.* New York and Cambridge: Cambridge University Press.

Yoshihara, M. (2003). *Embracing the east: white women and American orientalism.* New York and Oxford: Oxford University Press.

3333333

3333333333333

3333

Zerubavel, E. (1980). If Simmel were a fieldworker: On formal sociological theory and analytic field research. *Symbolic Interaction 3*, 25–33.

Zerubavel, E. (1991). *The fine line: Making distinctions in everyday life*. New York: Free Press.

Zerubavel, Y. (1995). *Recovered roots: Collective memory and the making of Israeli national tradition*. Chicago: University of Chicago Press.

Zhou, M. (1997). Growing up American: The challenge confronting immigrant children and children of immigrants. *Annual Review of Sociology 23*, 63–95.

Index

www.ingramcontent.com/pod-product-compliance
Lightning Source LLC
Chambersburg PA
CBHW062134040426
42335CB00039B/2109